BECAUSE I AM

JACKIE
MILLAR

Jackie Millar

BECAUSE I AM

JACKIE MILLAR

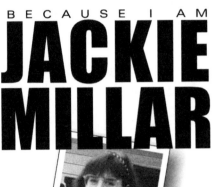

The amazing story of Jackie, shot execution style and left for dead – her miraculous recovery and her brave, new life dedicated to the end of violence

By JACKIE MILLAR and JUDITH GWINN ADRIAN

GOLDEN™
(THE PRESS)
A Division of GMG Golden Media Group

Because I Am Jackie Millar
Text copyright © 2007 by Jackie Millar and Judith Gwinn Adrian

First published in the USA in 2007 by
Golden (The Press)
A Division of GMG Golden Media Group
PO Box 17103
Encino, CA 91416
818-708-9488 • 877-GOLDNDJ
Visit our website at www.GoldenThePress.com

Lyrics to Jackie's Song reprinted with permission from:
A Hard Day S Write Music, Careers BMG Music, EMI Blackwood Music
Ensign Music, Lonesome Dove Music, Ticket To Ride Music

First trade paperback edition
10 09 08 07 1 2 3 4 5

ISBN 978-0-9797218-0-9

Cover and book design by Larry Girardi, Grafica Design Group
Crossed wheat sheaves have been used as a decorative element to accent selected text.
Wheat has symbolically represented the seasonal rebirth of life-sustaining crops,
and themes of resurrection and life throughout history,
an appropriate metaphor for Jackie's story.

Printed and bound in the USA

This book is dedicated to our children:
Denver, Molly, Sarah, Dan, Derek, Ann, Chad and Lisa.
We wish peace to Craig and Josh.

May they know love. May they know forgiveness.

CONTENTS

INTRODUCTION

Jackie talks. She talks with prisoners. They talk with her. And she speaks with middle school students, judges, church assemblies, high school students, District Attorneys, men's groups, prison guards, rehabilitation therapists, parole and probation officers, university students, police officers, women's groups, law students, and residents of halfway houses and group homes.

Her themes are essential: choices, forgiveness, and love.

Routinely Jackie is asked if she has written a book. Because of her traumatic brain injury, she could not do so alone. But together, we have recreated her story. I have added my observations on this remarkable woman, who in one breath tells me she has no memory of the execution-style shooting or subsequent events and, in the next, explains that she forgave the boys the minute they pulled the trigger sending a hollow-point bullet spiraling through her brain. Is this an impossible contradiction? We explore that question.

On November 4, 1995, Jackie had driven from Madison to Reedsburg to spend a weekend with her friend, John. She was alone in his house when two boys, Craig and Josh, walked in looking for keys to the red Honda parked in the open garage. They intended to steal the car. When Jackie asked what they were doing, the boys were surprised and confused. Without debate, they pulled out their stolen guns and told Jackie to lie down on the living room floor. She did exactly as she was told. They then covered her head with a pillow and shot her, point-blank, in the back of her head. They drove away in her car and later decided to try to get away with the crime by burning the car and returning to their homes.

The crime particulars are relatively straight-forward. But the transgression is shocking because of the randomness of the act. Haunting questions surface.

This book explores the impacts of this crime on Jackie, her family, friends and the larger community. We unearth who Jackie was before the shooting – her mix of shyness and confidence, her trusting nature and playful sense of humor – and explore any propensity to forgive. We delve into how she was physically and emotionally changed by what she calls *the accident*. And ultimately we examine her responses to the crime: her forgiveness and subsequent restorative justice work.

Jackie and I traveled to interview many of the people affected by the shooting. We began our journey by talking with Peggy, the grief counselor who met with Jackie's former co-workers at Lakeside Association Services (owned by the Wisconsin Medical Society). We went to that business to talk with Kathy and Lisa who had worked directly with Jackie. How had her associates responded to the shocking crime?

Who was Jackie before the shooting? We interviewed her ex-husband, Mark, and her ex-mother-in-law, Mary. We talked by phone with Mike, Mark's cousin, who wrote the country song that Jackie uses in her local and national presentations.

We talked with Barb, Jackie's long-time support worker and "broker," or advocate. What were Jackie's struggles as she moved beyond her physical and emotional traumas – her traumatic brain injury?

As we probed the crime itself and the people affected, we drove from Madison to Reedsburg, to the house where the shooting occurred. We interviewed John, Jackie's friend, and stood on the spot where she was shot. We talked about how Jackie can hate a place while caring deeply for its inhabitants. We spoke with Butch, the Sauk County Sheriff who led the investigation of the case.

We visited the University of Wisconsin Hospital and Clinics where Jackie lived for months during her rehabilitation.

Jackie's family agreed to talk with us and we interviewed her sons, Derek and Chad. What did the crime mean to these young men, only a couple of years older than the boys who shot their mother? We talked with Jackie's sister, Pam, and began to see more fully the range of people deeply affected by this crime.

And then we interviewed, by letter, the boys who shot Jackie. What were they thinking? Why did they shoot Jackie? Craig was 16 years old at the time of the shooting and Josh was 15. Both are in adult prison. She visits the boys yearly and they exchange letters regularly.

Jackie states that she loves these boys.

Amid the interviews, we have chapters that reveal Jackie's thoughts on a variety of subjects. Does she fear? What does traumatic brain injury feel like from the inside? How does she live with her abilities and disabilities? What about sporadic depression and even thoughts of suicide? Jackie describes her "Pity Parties for One." And, we talk about her forgiveness – the reality that most surprises her audiences. Where within Jackie did her immediate forgiveness come from?

I observed Jackie speaking to juveniles and inmates. We traveled first to the Dane County Juvenile Jail where she talked to youth. At a secured juvenile correctional facility where young men are incarcerated, I saw their responses to Jackie's story. We drove to Moose Lake and Willow River, two minimum security prisons in Minnesota, where Jackie talked to hundreds of men. Her presentations brought tears in each site. Jackie says, *They see their victims in me.* We heard from inmates about what Jackie's talks and connections meant to them. We talked with an ex-inmate.

Jackie makes a difference in inmates' lives. That is evident from their thoughtful questions and their visible shock at her ability to forgive the boys who shot her.

And last, Jackie and I stood alone in a vacant Marquette University classroom, prior to another of her presentations. In her uncensored spoken words, I heard the inner conversations she so often has as she struggles with her disabilities and lives her desire to seize each day and make a difference in this world.

Much of what is recorded in this book is in the speakers' words from the interviews, letters and emails. We have not grammatically edited the comments, though some are abridged. Our goal has been to capture the sweep of one crime and the ways it affected so many people's lives. Jackie will make this book available to inmates and students as she continues her restorative justice work and her presentations. Our hope is that it will stir reflective thoughts about choices, forgiveness and love.

How would you react, awakening from the shadowy space
of a drug-induced coma, to find your life was forever changed because
you had been the victim of a crime over which you had no control?

Vengeful? Hate-filled? Forgiving?

This is the story of Jackie Millar's awakening and choices.

I have made the right decision.
You and I will write a book, a true story about the accident
and the love and the forgiveness that has and is still being shown.

– Jackie Millar, June 1, 2006

WRITING JOURNAL

Jackie and I met when four graduate students in my course on change and transition took a short-cut in their hour-long class presentation on a significant societal issue. They engaged Jackie to speak. The students' ingenuity earned them a lack-luster grade because they introduced Jackie and stood back while she talked. But I became fascinated with Jackie's story, her reactions and her subsequent decisions related to the waves of changes she faced and faces in her life. She has spoken to students in my change course every semester since then, for years now.

It took a year of sporadic discussions before Jackie agreed to this collaborative writing. She did not want to further hurt her sons by bringing up old pain, she told me. But then her sons agreed to the book. I understood the reluctance superficially then. Many months and interviews later, it is far more clear. Jackie's life was fundamentally and irreparably altered by *the accident*. So were the lives of those surrounding her.

I see the courage it has taken for her to allow this story to be written. If my brain was stripped and polished so only snippets of memories stuck, would I trust a relative stranger to gaze in? Would I hide my differences? My fears?

Why does she risk? She answers. She says she has no patience for inconsequential events. Her time is limited.

MAY, 2006

A gardener is planting burnt orange marigolds and hot pink petunias in the circular space in front of Jackie's apartment building. We are meeting for the first time to begin work on this book. Jackie announces she is going to keep me at a distance. She won't let me in to her psyche or give me hugs. It is an inauspicious start to the project and odd since we have known each other for years, albeit formally, through Jackie's presentations to my classes.

In meetings to come, I pressure her in only one way. Each time as I leave, I give her a squeeze on her left shoulder. Not a quick touch; a real *shoulder hug*. A repetitious, meaningful and safe touch.

JULY, 2006

Jackie again speaks to one of my classes. Her presentation is quite different and I am surprised. She starts the same way, with an audio tape of spliced television newscasts giving information on the accident. She talks about what happened, who was involved, and where everyone is now. Then she asks for questions, and mixed in with the answers are many details from the stories and information we are learning from the interviews.

Our journey through the accident is creating (or triggering) memories for her. The information is satisfying the need to fill memory gaps – what she once called the *burden of her dullness*. I wonder how many times the gaps have been filled over the course of nearly eleven years but recognize that the question is irrelevant because the hunger to clarify the details is Jackie's burning passion.

After the class, I stand with her as we wait for her taxi. We chat and laugh and joke about some, now shared, stories. Our relationship is deepening. The yellow cab drives down the hill and we move toward the curb. Jackie surprises me by stopping, turning, and giving me a long, full hug – what a reporter referred to as one of her *signature hugs*.

OCTOBER, 2006

More and more Jackie seems to trust me. She asks questions about my life: my family and especially about my sister and the muscle degenerative disease that weakens her body but rarely her spirit.

I continue to respect Jackie's need for independence, not responding for her when others assume a woman with a white cane cannot answer.

NOVEMBER 4, 2006
ELEVENTH ANNIVERSARY OF THE ACCIDENT

Jackie and I go out for an early dinner this warm November Saturday. Sarah introduces herself as our server and Jackie orders a bacon cheeseburger. She then asks about the side dishes. Sarah opens the menu and points. With a smile, Jackie rests her hand on Sarah's arm and says, *I am legally blind and cannot see what you are indicating.*

On Sarah's next visit to our table, she again apologizes. *I went back and told the other servers I had made such a fool of myself.*

Jackie shakes her head. *I work so very hard at fitting in and hiding my differences. That you did not notice was wonderful for me.* She continues. *I am legally blind. I cannot use the right side of my body. And today is the eleventh anniversary of the day of the accident – the day I was shot.*

Twenty minutes later, clutching the black plastic folder with our bill in it and ignoring the chaos in the restaurant, Sarah hesitantly says, *I just have to ask how you got shot.*

It was for my car. Two boys wanted to steal my car and I interrupted them. They took me back inside the house and had me lie on the carpet, covered my head with a pillow, and then one of them shot me in the back of my head.

Sarah's eyes tear up. *And they just left you there?*

Yes. They left me for dead.

I am studying about brain injuries right now, Sarah explains. *I will write about you for my course.*

That is good. My name is Jackie. Jackie Millar. And I am healed. I have forgiven. I am healed from the inside and I would like to give you a hug.

Sarah leans down for her hug. She smiles, visibly warmed.

Apologetically she fumbles leaving the bill, seemingly thinking Jackie should not have to pay. We tip well.

When we are settled in the car and I have handed Jackie's Handicapped parking tag back to her, she says, *I so enjoyed talking with Sarah. She is about the same age the boys were. I do celebrate this day. I do. After all, this is the day I met Craig and Josh.*

GRIEF COUNSELOR • PEGGY

Surprisingly often, a student in my class will tell me she or he has met Jackie. Most have met her professionally because they work in the University of Wisconsin Hospital Intensive Care or Rehabilitation units where Jackie was a celebrity of sorts. In Peggy's case, she was the grief counselor called in to coach Jackie's co-workers following the shooting.

Excitement confounds Jackie's injured brain
and as we leave the classroom after a presentation to my class, she says,
*I just met the street walker…I don't want to call her a street walker…
after I was hurt my co-workers…*

The grief counselor?, I ask.

Yes, Jackie clarifies using a mnemonic:
Grief counselor. G…grief. C…counselor. Grief counselor.

A few weeks later we interview Peggy.

Peggy remembers, *When I think back to it, I remember being in shock after hearing about the shooting on the news. My thought even to this day is how could anyone do that?* Peggy turns to Jackie as we sit in a private restaurant booth and says, *I remember you being in such critical condition and everyone being so concerned about you. The next day I was called by an employee from Lakeside Association Services where you had worked. I said yes to a debriefing with your former co-workers.*

In response to Jackie's question about what a debriefing entails, Peggy explains, *Everyone who knows the victim or is involved with the accident is invited. I create a safe environment. We have this space to talk; we do not need to worry about getting back to work. No one leaves during the session. We are not looking at how we could have prevented the event but at how we feel about what happened.*

First we clarify the facts. After that, we go around and people tell their experience of the event. How was it for them? What are their memories? Generally it comes to a natural end after everyone has had a chance to talk and debrief. And then I talk about normal reactions to critical incidents and what each person can do for their physical and emotional care.

At your debriefing, Jackie, I was nervous; frankly scared. It was a different setting. The event was so horrible.

Jackie listens attentively. Her right arm won't cooperate and she unthinkingly drags it across the table and pulls it to her chest, saying, *It is something else to think that the employees had come there for me; had come to grieve for me.*

Peggy continues. *They had to bring in more chairs. There was not enough room for everyone. There was an update on Jackie's medical condition: some facts from the intensive care unit. Someone had spoken to the hospital at noon and they were slightly hopeful. There was some sign – a change of blood pressure – something to hang on to.*

But then, what was so different was that after the person said what had happened, everybody wanted to speak at the same time. How could they do that? How could they do that? There was this immense anger that to this day I have never experienced again in a group. There was shock, but there was immediate anger.

Your co-workers wouldn't move off of their anger. Most of the people were crying through the whole thing. Women and men. Both were crying. They really knew you. It wasn't just a colleague, it was a friend. You did not deserve it. That is why they were so mad.

I am worried that Jackie is becoming distraught. Her head is down. I nod to Peggy hoping she will pause with her intense story. She does.

Jackie slowly enunciates; her words separated like beads on a string. *I was so trusting. What did they talk about?*

Peggy continues. *I had never experienced adults being so angry. Then I eventually realized I was not going to be able to move them beyond the anger. So I took them to talking about what they could control. How could we use that energy that came with their anger? What could they do? What could they do for your sons?*

At the end of debriefings, I like to try to pull it together – offer them resources and what symptoms to expect. This was such a mess. I did not feel like I had helped them at all; like I had moved them. I walked out feeling very very drained because of the incredible sadness and the madness and the scared. I didn't know what to have them hope for.

You did make a difference, Jackie consoles. *You gave them their chance to say they were mad and upset.*

STATE MEDICAL SOCIETY • KATHY AND LISA

Several days later, Jackie and I arrive at the Lakeside Association Services building at the same time. I watch her crawl out of the taxi, pulling her wheeled and slightly shabby black suitcase behind her carrying the stash of pictures and letters and videos she uses in presentations. Her gait is faster and she seems to walk more steadily than usual, although her right foot continues to curl inward. She presses it flat with each measured step. I stop watching as I catch up remembering that, with the new medical pump now sewn inside her abdomen, Jackie may not be in pain; not in pain for the first time in eleven years.

With her permission, I take her suitcase and we climb the stairs together.

Jackie greets the receptionist and asks for Kathy and Lisa, her former co-workers. The receptionist calls on her state-of-the-art office phone system. During the slight delay, Jackie walks into the once familiar building. The receptionist is torn between her responsibility to control visitors and her tether to the phone system. Visually fussing, the receptionist gives in to the technology as I follow Jackie down the hall, smiling at her spunk.

Was your office near here? I ask.

Downstairs.

Clearly memories are triggering. To the receptionist's relief, Kathy and Lisa arrive and, after hugs, redirect us to a newly redecorated and unfamiliar library area. The table is dustless. The books are politically correct and I notice the large section on financial management. Even though it is Friday, I see no *business casual* in this organization.

After catching up on respective family stories, the talk turns to reminiscences.

Kathy comments, *You changed a lot the last year you worked here; you had been the shy quiet one in the corner. The last conference you were in charge of, you got up in front of a group of exhibitors and gave a speech. My mouth dropped to the floor.*

Reaching for memories, I ask why. *Why were you changing, Jackie?*

I think I wanted to get out of my shell. I am very brazen and I do everything off the top of my head. Jackie taps her chest proudly. *But I do everything at least once. I started to like it. I told myself I was important; I had important thoughts.* Jackie smiles, impishly.

We didn't even know when you were getting a divorce. You never said a word to anybody. I just remember you got some beautiful roses one day. Was it your anniversary? *Those beautiful flowers sat there all weekend. Someone asked about your husband and you simply said,* I'm getting a divorce, *just like you'd say I am going out for a walk.*

It was very private for me, Jackie muses, *I can remember calling my friend Deb, the day we had the finalization – the day we met the judge. I said,* It's over. *It was sad and it was happy; it was everything. I just couldn't get over, I was divorced.*

The girl talk continues.

One of my fondest memories is when you would get personal phone calls and you would start whispering and turn your back to everyone. So we would all go and stand next to your desk. One time you had on a dress with a long tie on the back. While you were talking, we tied you to your chair. We picked on you horribly. All of that was part of you coming out of your shell.

You would say, Go away! *But we would hug you. We even held your arms down to hug you. You did not like it.*

Jackie nods heartily.

Do you remember the practical joke we played on you with your wall partitions? You needed such privacy. So on March 31, we stayed late, getting ready for an April Fools' trick. We took your partitions and hid them. The next morning we waited for you to come in. You looked all around and said, Where's my walls? *We laughed and laughed.*

I needed my space, Jackie protests, clearly enjoying the banter.

The teasing tones are still there all these years after the accident. The laughter belies the formality of this place and its dress code.

Suddenly, poignantly and without preface, Jackie says, *I think it is funny that you have my former job, Lisa. Funny, I don't mean it funny ha ha. It is ironic. I remember you because you were…I don't want to say like me, because everyone is individual…but I could understand you.*

Silence surrounds this moment as we all quietly acknowledge that Jackie has moved on and will never work in this high pressure world again.

Kathy breaks the silence. *I got the phone call. I don't know who called me, but I got it on a Sunday. You just don't believe what you are hearing. I called our co-workers; they all had the same response,* You are lying!

We came in on Monday and Jackie was scheduled to have three conferences coming up that week. Some of the conference materials were in her car and had been burned with the car. She was so organized that we were able to go to her computer and put those conferences together. It was good that we had something to do so we did not fall apart. Turning to Lisa, she says, *Do you remember? We sat on the floor. We didn't sit at our desks. We put Jackie's conferences together for her.*

Lisa adds, *I remember how I found out about it. I walked in the lobby and Pat said to me,* Did you hear about Jackie? *I said,* Oh, what did she do now? *I was thinking she was going to say Jackie was going on a vacation to Europe or doing more grocery shopping in the middle of the night. There was that disbelief. My dumb question was,* Is she OK?

The phone rang all day. People were saying, That isn't our Jackie is it? *One of the heads of the company said,* We need to get you some counseling. *We said,* Just leave us alone today; we have work to get done. *We were mourning in our own way; I didn't leave my space.*

Again a pause and then a return to an easier subject, *I do think you were happier when you could get mad at us.* All laugh.

Jackie stays in the past, *I think that this building has a lot of good memories for me; besides my kids it was number two in my life and I think that you…I thank you for being in that part of my life. I couldn't have had many first things in my life had it not been for you. I got to give, for the first time; to do what I wanted to do.*

The conversation is fading. Someone tries to revive it by asking about a specific conference event but the conversation ends with Jackie's final shake of her head and a comment. *I wish I could remember. I don't remember a lot of things, but I remember you guys.* Jackie shakes her head slowly.

We say good-bye and leave.

I give Jackie a ride to the City-County Building where she is again speaking to youth in the juvenile jail. I accompany her. Her days are rich.

FEAR

As part of our process, Jackie and I have discussed some specific topics. The fear she feels is one of these. I am doing the final editing of this book in the Mexican Caribbean on Isla Mujeres. There is no glass on the windows of my room, only louvers. As my father used to say, the spaces between these louvers are *wide enough to throw a cat through*. I think about how Jackie would be afraid to sleep here alone. Her sister, Pam, and others have hinted at the ongoing fear Jackie lives with since the accident.

I moved into an unsecured apartment building because I had to find out whether I would be scared or not scared. All the supportive people with their great intentions couldn't help me. You take a child and she will learn by her mistakes. I know that. They have to find out for themselves; I had to find out. This apartment was on the first floor. It wasn't security locked. And I was scared.

I ask, *What were you frightened of?*

I was scared that someone would get me. Would hurt me. Would kill me. I felt with every fiber of my being that someone was going to get me. It wasn't about the accident. I had it generally. That someone would get me. I jumped at every noise. I had every light on. I would have a chair up against a locked door. But it was always in my head that someone's out there. That is one thing that Craig and Josh gave me.

It is better being in this secure apartment building now, on the third floor. The fear doesn't go away but I don't let it overtake me. I have gotten so I will leave the sliding screen door open during the day. For me, that is monumental. But at night, I lock the door. I lock the screen and the storm door. About 9:30 or 10 at night, I put my latch on in addition to the deadbolt lock I put on when I come in the apartment. I don't let my guard down. You know, people will tell me, Oh you are safe in there. *I am never safe. I am never safe.*

I interrupt Jackie and ask, *Do you remember if you were afraid of anything before the accident?*

There was nothing I was scared of before. I loved thunderstorms. My door was unlocked. I would go grocery shopping at 3:30 in the morning if I felt like it. It was a peaceful country I thought I lived in.

Let's try to go inside the fear, I suggest to Jackie. *What does it feel like inside of you?*

In the unsecured apartment, it took me hours to fall asleep. I would hear every sound that there was. The creaking. The doors slamming. The cars. I would hear everything. But then after three or four hours I'd fall asleep only to wake up again in another three hours. I'd have to try to go to sleep all over again. I would have to get up and check the doors and check the windows. It is foolish – well, it isn't foolish for me. It is the accident's damage on me. I have had to – have had to – have had to... Jackie struggles to find the right word. *I will always have fear but it is manageable now. When I first had the fear, it wasn't manageable.*

It was like...it could happen all over again. Jackie closes her eyes and sits quietly. *You know I want to say,* Darn Craig, darn Josh. *I was a peace-loving individual. I wouldn't hurt anybody.*

There was one time I lived in an apartment, the Normandy Apartments. I decided on a test for me. I decided that I had to find out if I could walk home when it was not dark, but half-way dark. I did. It worked. I try out my different things and I walked it in half-darkness.

I ask, *Why test yourself?*

For me to find out if I was strong enough to handle my fears. I wanted to get back Jackie – it doesn't mean I wasn't afraid. I was. But I conquered the fear. I think that I conquered my fear for me to go on.

FAMILY • MARK AND MARY

Mark and Mary, Jackie's ex-husband and mother-in-law.

I have arrived at Jackie's apartment before her ex-mother-in-law and her ex-husband. We will interview them today about who Jackie was as a younger woman and about their memories of the accident.

From the apartment entryway area I hear, *Hi Sweetie.*

Mark and Mary are at the door. They are a well dressed, attractive pair. Mary has professionally styled grey hair and an even tan. Her open-toed shoes expose a chic toe ring. Mark wears a black tee shirt with a sports emblem on it and new athletic shoes, also black. His tan slacks are pressed.

We met in high school, Mark explains. *Jackie was working in Manchester's Department Store in gift wrapping and I was a stocker for the Store for Homes. She was less gregarious then; more reserved. She was not a hugger...*

Everyone hugs and kisses in our family, Mary interjects. *Jackie was uncomfortable with that.*

Mark continues, *Jackie was shy and naïve. We were out walking one night in high school. There was a half moon and Jackie wondered where the other half went.*

Mark and Jackie, early in their relationship.

Mary adds, *Jackie got involved with my son and nephew when they were all playing bridge. She wasn't a great player initially and if you questioned her plays, she would go into the bathroom to cry. She looked at the comments as criticism. She was very touchy and quite sensitive. But she got to be a good player.*

Mark adds, *We got married in 1970 and our sons were born in March of 1974 and October of 1976. We had a lot in common; we were both homebodies even before the kids were born. She was so selfless. Always thinking of the other person. She was the perfect daughter, the perfect wife, the perfect mother.*

Smiling, Mary adds, *Jackie is a totally different person now. We like her better! She has a different kind of humor now than she did before the accident. She can laugh at herself.*

Mark explains that their boys were ill all the time and it was quite stressful. *Jackie literally moved into the hospital when the boys were sick; especially with Chad. Derek had a seizure in 2nd or 3rd grade when he had encephalitis.*

Fourth grade, Jackie corrects.

The discussion turns to the illnesses Mark and Jackie's boys experienced: *Gamma Globulin injections for autoimmune disease…three shots at a time with big needles. It was a three to five hour deal every three weeks. Jackie was always a very, very, very protective mother,* Mary explains. *She had a stubborn streak and would not let anyone else help with the boys.*

I muse inwardly thinking the stubborn streak became a survival streak.

No one touches my kids, Jackie exclaims.

You're a mess, Mary offers gently, referring to Jackie's very recent surgery. *Does your foot feel better?*

A little bit here and there.

We move on to the subject of Mark's umpiring and refereeing for basketball and football games. *I am a huge, huge sports fan. It was part of the problem with the marriage. I wasn't always around.* Jackie and Mark were married for 20 years and then divorced 5 years before the accident. *We took the boys on two trips. The Badgers were playing at LSU in Baton Rouge. The Badgers got beat. And another time I was umpiring in Florida. It was a working vacation. We went to Disney World. I think we had a good time,* he adds, looking at the back of Jackie's chair for confirmation.

Mark and Jackie, prior to their divorce.

Mary agrees that Mark is a huge sports fan. *Over the edge, more than most men. Sports are his life. He referees and umpires all over the country now.*

And then we agree to talk about the accident. As with others who lived through this time, the details are crisp, clear. There is no hesitation. The discussion begins with the date, *It was November 4, 1995.*

Mark explains, *I was home and was sleeping when a call came at about 12:30pm. I was told,* Jackie is on her way to the University of Wisconsin Hospital by med flight. Somebody should be there. *I called Mom who told me to pick her up and we would go together. When we entered the hospital and asked for Jackie, they wouldn't let us in her room. They knew I was her ex-husband but did not know that I wasn't the person who had hurt her.*

My daughter's mother-in-law worked at the hospital and explained that it was OK to let us in, Mary adds.

We knew Jackie's marriage and birth dates.

Jackie's face was swollen and there were tubes all over. She was in a pressure suit. We were not given any good news; the prognosis was not good, says Mary, her foot swinging.

The trauma is embedded deeply and clearly in Mary and Mark's memories. *That first night, our whole family was there. There were twelve of us. One of us was with Jackie all the time for six weeks while she was in the drug-induced coma and then waking up after that.*

What were your feelings, I ask.

Horror, Mark and Mary say in unison.

When she was coming to, we did not have much hope. She was such a great person. We always go to why.

As she began to get better, she had to relearn so many things; she was like a baby. There were years of physical therapy. When did you end physical therapy, Jackie?

November 3, 1996.

Laughing, I say, *Approximately?*

We talk about the press coverage. *The press questions were constant.* Mary indicates a span of about three feet with her hands. *I have video tapes of all the news reports. And I kept a scrap book of all of the newspaper coverage and other events. Christmas was coming and John raises Christmas trees – beautiful Fraser*

trees. He donated one to the Bank of Verona where Jackie had banked. My daughter and I decorated it. The bank set up a memorial and donor's names went on the tree. I have pictures if you want to see them. There was a ceremony when the tree was cut. At that point we did not know what was going to happen. We were soliciting money for Derek and Chad's education, and for Chad's medical bills. Both sons were interviewed on TV.

Derek and Chad looking at the Christmas tree from John's farm honoring their mother and raising funds for their continuing education.

Some moments of silence settle in the room and then Mary adds that Jackie was always part of their family. *She came to family events after the divorce.*

The chair Jackie sits in faces the television, which means she is positioned with her back to Mary and Mark, who sit on the couch and computer chair respectively. Jackie's comments are not directed toward anyone in particular, but she enters this conversation saying, *I remember the day we got the divorce. It was sad. I was leaving the man I had loved for 20 years. Of course there was sadness.*

Mark, speaking to the back of Jackie's chair, adds, *We used the same attorney and agreed on equal custody and on what to share. I kept the house and paid her half of the value. I wanted the kids to be able to keep their friends in the neighborhood. Jackie lived close by. It was a simple, congenial situation. The judge said it was the most congenial divorce he had ever seen. It was good for the kids. There was no fighting so it was easy for us all to stay together as a family.*

Mary has an appointment to meet friends for a movie so she and Mark depart. After the door is closed, Jackie sits down heavily in her chair, tired from the interviews. She is distracted for a minute by the chatter of squirrels outside the open patio door. She says, *Mary is the salt of the earth. She has been there for me. And I think the world of Mark. A divorce doesn't end my feelings.*

SONG • MIKE

Mike, songwriter.

Mike is Jackie's ex-husband's cousin. As a record producer, he has written and recorded a song for Jackie.[1] After we interview him by phone, he emails additional stories from California from his early memories of Jackie and Mark together.

I came home to Beloit, Wisconsin, on emergency leave from Vietnam on May 2, 1970. Mark and Jack (as I've always called Jackie) were planning to be married the first part of June and Mark had asked me to be his best man, but since I was due back in Vietnam the day of their wedding I suggested he go with his long-time friend Rick. However, just before I boarded the plane at Fort Lewis, Washington, my orders were changed to Fort Sheridan, Illinois. I called Mark to tell him. Rick had already been fitted for his tux so we all agreed it would be only fair for Rick to be best man. However, we decided to surprise Jack and let her just see me at the wedding. So, 'here comes the bride' down the isle with her father. The look of disbelief when I caught her eye made us all laugh.

As Jackie was recovering and going through her long therapy, Mike wrote Jackie's Song (his lyrics are italicized):

Jackie's Song [2]

I didn't hear the sirens that car-jacking day
I was so far gone I couldn't even pray
Blinding flash exploding sound told me to lay down and die

---

[1] *Mike has produced many recordings with long-time friend and multi-Grammy winner, Jimmie Haskell ("Bridge Over Troubled Waters," "Ode To Billy Jo," and the Chicago tune, "If You Leave Me Now"). Jimmie also arranged and conducted the strings for "Jackie's Song."*

[2] *The song's real story is who wrote the other lyrics and the melody/music. It's like Who's Who in country and pop music. You'll quickly see that "Jackie's Song" has quite a pedigree and was no accident. The first is Sonny LeMaire, former Exile bass player and writer. Sonny has written 10 #1 songs, several for Exile, but many for country acts including the recent Diamond Rio hit, "Beautiful*

But it's always darkest just before dawning
I'm finally facing a brand new morning
I've been through the fire and I know that I can survive

Chorus

I didn't know my own strength
Just how strong I could be
Then I came face to face
With someone stronger than me
Lord I learned to stand tall
And to carry the weight
I can't believe that I've come this far
I didn't know my own strength

You said you'd love me forever more
But you never even darkened my hospital door
In your letter you told me now I'd just be holding you down
I prayed let me die but a voice said, "You're needed"
Never in my life have I been so *completed*
Helping others in turn is helping me to turn this around

Bridge

Just when I thought that I could not take it
I found the power inside to make it

Referring to the lyrics, Mike explains, *I wrote the signature lyrics before I knew the full story. In an odd way, the lyric is a kind of telecommunication. I did not know that Jack felt she had talked with God before I wrote the song. I did not know that the fellow she was dating from Colorado was going to drop her after the accident. The lyrics are intensely personal. I was afraid to let Jack hear the song for years so it just sat on my shelf. It was recorded in 1999 but it was 2 or 3 years later*

Mess." Next is Bobbie Cryner. A recording artist on both Epic and MCA, she turned to songwriting scoring a number of hits including Trisha Yearwood's "Real Live Woman." And finally, the most well known of all, Kent Blazy, who with Garth Brooks co-wrote Garth's first #1, "If Tomorrow Never Comes," (and since then Kent Blazy songs have appeared on every Garth Brooks album, except one).

before her family and I felt it was OK to let her hear it. A family birthday party seemed like the right time (though I personally couldn't attend the party, my aunt Mary and I worked out the details).

As Mike talks over the phone, Jackie is standing at the sliding glass door looking out. Birds sing outside. Her back is to me. She stands straight, remembering perhaps. As with the other stories we have heard, she cannot get enough information. I have the sense that she is able to hold the stories for just a few minutes before parts of them dribble away.

Mike continues, *Jackie listened to the record at that birthday party. She cried. And then she asked that it be played again. And again. And again. It so touched her. It epitomized what she had gone through. It captured the emotion that she could feel even though she could not remember in words. Jackie and her accident are always just below the surface for those of us who love her.*

Jackie breaks in to the story to say she appreciates what Mike has said.

I know, Mike responds.

As so often happens, Mike addresses Jackie to ask if she remembers this. Slowly she says, *No.*

He explains, *There are a lot of things I have told Jackie. I would ask her if she remembered such and such and a year later, she wouldn't remember. The damage to her memory was not a one time thing. It is a hit and miss thing, even today. It is almost like she has a form of Alzheimer's. She will remember a lot of things, but some of the subtler nuance things, leave.*

Jackie stands, shaking her head. Resigned?[3]

---

[3] Update from Mike on August 21, 2006: *Tomorrow I master a new album. It's a compilation album entitled: Rx for Lonely Housewives & Desperate Lovers. One of the cuts will be the instrumental version of "Jackie's Song" with some quotes from part of the 1999 Milwaukee Sentinel article about Jack as well as a few of my lyrics to the song in the liner notes, just to give the audience an introduction to Jackie and a taste of what's to come…we hope.*

SUPPORT WORKER & BROKER • BARB

Jackie continues to line up family and friends to talk with us. Each person holds another piece of her puzzle. *It is through everyone that a clear picture of who I am comes,* she explains to me. Barb comes into the apartment. I can hear the women greeting each other well before they enter the living room. Barb has been Jackie's Support Worker and Broker since September, 1996, when she was first released from Rehabilitation and living with her son, Chad. Barb's job was to help with grocery shopping, meal preparation and anything else Jackie couldn't handle on her own. Barb is employed by United Cerebral Palsy of Greater Dane County, Wisconsin, a non-profit organization.

Hello. I'm here, Barb calls.

Barb is an attractive woman wearing turquoise beads at her throat that set off her tan. We shake hands. Her hand is slim but strong. Jackie has moved the computer chair toward her recliner and the guest chair I sit in, creating a circle for the three of us.

Was I childlike when I was recovering? Jackie asks. Her continual craving to fit together the puzzle pieces is openly part of the conversations now.

No, never, Barb replies, facing Jackie fully. *You were strong-headed, strong-willed, and on a mission. I see shyness in you in public places, like restaurants. I don't see it in you when you speak to groups. You've gotten better and better at speaking. And better and better at dealing with your disabilities.*

Barb knows to remain silent as Jackie forms her sentence. *More strong-willed...that is a good word for me.* Jackie smiles.

Continuing, Barb says, *Early on, Jackie didn't trust me. I would come in. She would order me around. I would do what she wanted and she would say,* OK, you can leave now. *She did not* want *to need help. I tried not to take it personally, but I was not sure if I should continue to come back during those early visits.*

Without hesitation, Jackie interjects, *And you should not have taken it personally. I had just had a horrendous crime take place at me. I was trying to make sense of the accident but I could not.*

Barb reflects on the beginning of their relationship. *I remember reading a book to you; that is when we first really connected. The woman in the book was brain damaged. Her name was Jackie. She was in an accident. She also speaks in public. She was hijacked on a plane, shot, and thrown on the tarmac to die. You listened to the story and then you would sit up and say,* That's me. That's me.

Barb's stories come faster. *One day Jackie called me and said,* I can see! *After reacting the way Jackie hoped I would, I slowly realized she was teasing me and we began to recognize we had a similar sense of humor.*

Jackie smiles easily. *Barb is my support broker and friend. She has my friendship first and then she is my support broker. I'll tell her stories to see if she believes me.* I'm getting married. I'm walking with a walker. *If she says,* Yeah, right, *then I know she got the joke.*

She will call me at work with her jokes, Barb explains.

Oh, it's not true…ha, ha, ha. It picks me up. I am able to say I don't hurt. Jackie smiles crookedly, playfully.

Barb laughs and moves to a more serious topic. *One thing I've watched change is her willingness to embrace what has happened to her. It has taken a long time to let herself feel the anger and sadness and pain of what happened. It is still coming out. Sometimes I would get a call and she would admit to having a bad day. I'd tell her it is OK to have feelings about this.*

Barb describes the restlessness that was part of Jackie's recovery. *She was learning what had happened to her and she was learning to be a new Jackie. From rehab, Jackie moved back to her condo in Verona. Her son, Chad, was with her and was devastated. He was in bed all day, sleeping, depressed. Jackie decided to sell the condo and move to Madison where transportation was easier. She moved into a locked unit [an apartment with security locks] in this apartment building. After about a year there was a phone call.* I want to move to the east side, *Jackie would assert. When I asked why, she said,* Why? I don't know. I just want to see what it is like to live on the east side.

Jackie moved about once a year and every time she moved, she would say, It is mine, all mine! *A year later she would call me and say,* I want to move. To the west side. *She has lived in three different apartments on this block.*

Laughing, I ask Jackie why she wanted to move all the time and am struck by her answer.

I felt, I can't go and drive a car. I can't take a picture like I used to. But I can move. It is how I am. Shaking her head, she continues, *But now it's…I realize I can't move for the sake of moving. I think I will stay here. It is handy for me.*

We talk about Jackie's work and the two women remember a trip they took to a juvenile detention center for a speaking engagement.

Barb explains, *It was a rainy, cold, gray day. We went to the detention center and I passed through the metal detector. They do a wand on Jackie. They brought us into the mess hall and fed us prison lunch. It consisted of chicken soup, crackers and some kind of sandwich. We sat with the wardens. They put us in a van and took us to a chapel on top of a hill in the compound. They brought in about 50 young men who had committed horrendous crimes. They were hard core young men from inner cities and gangs. They filled the whole church.*

There were guards surrounding the group. Jackie started her presentation. She talked about her sons, the accident, her work, and what is wrong with her. She was doing fine when, in the middle of her speech, she walked over to me and said, I am going to be sick. *She turned around and walked to the other end of the room, paused, and vomited all over the floor. Everyone just sat there. The guys in uniform just stood there. I said,* Could someone please help her! *They went and got towels.* Is there a bathroom? Yes, downstairs.

Jackie had to walk down three flights of stairs to the basement. She had a lot of trouble with the stairs but she didn't want any help. I waited outside the door for a while and then went back upstairs. The men were still sitting there, staring. It was silent. The boys were standing, as they had been instructed, with their arms down like sticks at their sides. Jackie was still in the bathroom, so I went back down.

Should we leave?, *I ask her.*

Jackie announces, NO! We are not leaving. I wasn't finished. *There is thunder and lightening. The wind is blowing horribly.*

Jackie comes out of the bathroom stall and says, How do I get back up stairs? *I showed her the way and she walks up the stairs and right down the middle of the aisle to the front and finishes talking. She is white as a ghost. Finally she says,* I am finished, *flings open the door, and leaves. I follow her. The wind is crazy. The guards put us in a van and take us to the front gates. Jackie has another speaking engagement near the Wisconsin Dells that afternoon.* We should just go home, *I say to her.* Nope, *Jackie says.* We have reservations. *We get into the motel. She is still very sick. I take her to the meeting room. She talks and we go back to the motel. A few hours later, she wakes me up. It is 2 in the morning. She says,* Now we are going home.

I ask Jackie why.

I wanted to finish what I started. I finished the story. I may have had to sit down but I finished the story. I had to, you know, um, I have limited time. Barb doesn't like me to talk like this. But I have limited time. I can only speak to so many people. There are so many.

Barb finishes her story by talking about the juvenile offenders who write Jackie. *She gets hundreds of letters. These kids write Jackie about the crimes they have committed. They tell her things they won't tell their counselors. They trust Jackie with their stories. They trust a victim more than they trust those who are in the prison system to help them.*

TRAUMATIC BRAIN INJURY

TBI can cause a wide range of functional changes affecting thinking, sensation, language, or emotions.[4]

In what is becoming a pattern in our meetings now, Jackie skips any formal or even informal greetings or *how-r-you's*. She moves directly into our discussions, often before I can get the computer functioning fully! She is very focused.

Jackie reflects on her memory. *I would say that I am starting to remember. I laugh 'cause the doctors said it was two years I would remember and bang, that's*

---

[4] *Thinking (memory and reasoning); Sensation (touch, taste, and smell); Language (communication, expression, and understanding); and Emotion (depression, anxiety, personality changes, aggression, acting out, and social inappropriateness). http://www.cdc.gov/ncipc/tbi/Outcomes.htm*

it. But I practice, practice. You will see me singing. And you will see me talking to myself. It's the only way I know to get the practice in. It is the only way. I am OK about my eyes. They are legally blind. I am OK with that. But the talking… Jackie pauses with her hand to her mouth, half smiling. *I don't talk like I used to but I talk good. You will hear me say sometimes five words together. That is honestly good. I will never talk the same way I did ten years ago but I will talk better and better.*

It occurs to me that part of what we are recording in this writing are Jackie's current memories; not a bad reason to write this book.

Jackie is distracted on this visit. She switches topics and talks about her frustration at the written request she has received from one of the boys involved in the accident. He has asked if she plans to speak at his parole hearing; she feels he is asking her to speak in support of his early release.

She apologizes to me. *I am sorry that I vented with you yesterday. I needed time. I can sort through things, but slowly. It takes me a good 24 hours. I get my initial feeling, my impromptu…I have my impulsive actions. That is what you heard me do. I needed overnight; I need the peace to come over me to make the correct decision. Otherwise I can make some real doozie decisions. I don't know how to get out of a decision I've made. That's why I wait. I can make a split second decision, but oh boy, I don't know what I've gotten myself into. I am slow at seeing the right thing to do. Given time, doggone it, I think I make 90 to 95% good decisions.*

There is a quick emotional response. And then I calm down. I need to know the facts. I can't go to my sons. I can't go to my sister. I have to go inside myself and say, Calm down. *Give me the facts and I will make a decision. It's too often all of the emotions that get me into trouble. I want to get to the truth. The truth about whatever.*

I have put my feelings neatly in a cement booth, neatly in a cement booth. I don't want to be hurt again. So I cement them up neatly. They will never, except for my sons, be shown to anyone. I am telling you, I have told no one else.

The people I hug, it is physically the closest I've been to anybody. I have distance from my audiences. It is about twelve inches or more. I can feel my tentacles coming out when someone has overstepped without asking. I get this feeling like I want to back away. I can't see very well. Being blind is part of this. I am uneasy with a sudden movement. It is…I am worried that I won't see everything.

It's, Jackie pauses and shakes her head, *seeing a person walking down the street. You are worried that that person is going to say something to you. You know some-one can be talking to a person they have seen ahead of me and I worry thinking, Are they talking to me? It is me, it is me. I shouldn't be so worried about them. But I'm worried I will not acknowledge.*

I think that if I slow down I can be like who I was before. It may or may not be true; that is what I think.

THE ACCIDENT · JOHN

It has been almost exactly eleven years since the accident when Jackie and I drive the fifty-five miles north of Madison to Reedsburg. We are going to visit Jackie's friend, John, and the house where Jackie was shot; the house and tree farm she had gone to on November 4, 1995. She chats steadily while I simul-taneously drive and take notes on the tablet perched on my lap.

I am leery. I am leery. It seems like yesterday that all of this happened. I am angry at the house where it happened. The anger has to go someplace and it is easier to be angry at an inanimate object. I cannot be angry with the boys who shot me but I can be furious with a house. I can control my anger at a house. The crime is non-sensical; I cannot make sense of it. I struggle with that.

Jackie begins to explain the accident to me and I gently share that I know the story she is telling me. We laugh about aging and forgetting.

She reflects, *I admit I am brain injured. I blame the boys even when I know my forgetting has nothing to do with the accident; even when I know it is a sign that I'm getting older.*

Jackie is easily and pleasantly interruptible. I ask how she and John met.

I placed an impersonal ad…I mean a personal ad. We both liked outdoors, trees and flowers. He was the last person anyone would have picked for me, but we were instant friends and have been for 15 years. He is someone I could talk to. We would sit and talk for hours. We had spirited discussions. We could disagree but we never got angry. I like someone who holds a different point of view and who will let me have my perspective too. He would say, Jackie is honest. Before the accident, I was so trusting and people felt they had to take me under their wing so I wouldn't get hurt. John wasn't that way. He was just himself with me. He was John no matter what. I like that.

The day of the accident I was visiting John and his son. I was breaking up with my boyfriend and wanted someone to talk to.

Jackie pauses then says, smiling, *John will be using his best language with you today.*

I drive. Jackie talks. And then we turn off of Highway 12 for the last fourteen miles of our trip. Jackie becomes completely silent; like a plug has been pulled. She looks out the right side of the car, her head turned away from me. The ditches are heavy with blameless blue late summer Chicory. There is the first hint of color in the trees and red fringes on the Sumac. Wisconsin super sweet corn is for sale in roadside stands. One minute of silence. Two. Five. The only sounds are the hum of the engine and an occasional swallow from Jackie.

I ask, *You OK?*

She replies, *Yep.*

As we pull into Reedsburg the roadway opens to five full lanes. The commercial areas are set far back with parking lots facing the roadway. A jet airliner could land in this town entrance. I think about how the rugged beauty of this Wisconsin land has been bulldozed back to make room for commerce. Where is the *human scale* architects talk about, I wonder?

Jackie sits silently, pushing her right hand down on her thigh and flattening out the curling fingers.

She instructs me, *Turn right on County V. That is the street he lives on.*

As we drive into an older residential area of town, the human scale improves. The homes and trees are smaller and more inviting and yet I am thinking that this is the street the boys who shot Jackie walked down looking for a car to steal. We drive past the post office, the water tower, and the Reedsburg Brewery. The boys must have been cold that November 4th. It was ten or twelve blocks from the center of town to the high school and I remember that the boys hid their guns in the woods behind that school.

We continue to drive out of town. The road narrows as it winds into bucolic rural Wisconsin. White picket fences and a weeping willow frame a creek. We drive over the narrow bridge. There are wooden farm houses displaying American flags. Labor Day is coming. Queen Anne's Lace crowds the roadway.

Jackie is taking deep breaths.

This is it. Turn here, Jackie commands.

I turn into the driveway of a modest house. A honey wagon is leaving – the septic tank now clean – and we pull onto the grass to let it pass.

As we get close to the house, Jackie states, *This isn't it; the driveway should be on the left.*

We back out and as we leave, I glance in the rear view mirror seeing my tire tracks on the lawn. We drive. Thirty miles per hour; one mile, two miles.

Jackie sighs. *If I could see…Lighthouse Camp. That is good. Keep going. This is it; turn here.*

John and his friend Patty are in the garage and walk out to meet us. John is unshaven around his mustache. His longish curls stick out from his well worn red work cap. He extends a strong warm hand first to Jackie and then to me. I notice massive forearms; a working man's arms. Patty shakes hands with equal direct friendliness. We walk in through the garage which smells sweetly of ripening cantaloupe. I am thinking this is where the boys entered the house. We pass through the kitchen and again I'm thinking this is where the boys stood deciding which gun to use. The house is inseparable from the event and I begin to feel how Jackie can hate a place while caring deeply for its inhabitants.

John is a casual housekeeper. There are tidy stacks of papers and other things on many surfaces. The kitchen and hallway floors are covered in diamond-patterned gold linoleum. Ahead of us are the bedrooms and a bathroom. To the right is the living room; the walls pale yellow. The vacuumed gold carpet matches the linoleum. The furniture is Early American maple. The fabric on the matching couch and love seat sports generous yellow and orange flowers.

To set up the laptop computer, I slide over a half used roll of duct tape. Nearby is a Nutrition Action Healthletter on the topic of *Food Porn*. I see a TV Guide, a pen, a Wick assembly box, a tube of caulk, a phone, toothpicks, a coffee cup and a pile of magazines. In the corner to my right is a wooden bookcase with New Standard Encyclopedias lined up. Volumes 4, 10, 13, 6 and 9 are visible; the rest of the set is nearly covered by a lean Norfolk Island Pine. There is a wooden diamond shaped insert in the front door window. The drapes on the picture window are pale yellow and thin light reflects onto the large mustard colored glass lamp. The lawn outside is neatly mowed. A calendar with vegetables pictured on it is turned to September first, one day early. A Packers chair rests in the corner, near the towering Bowflex Xtreme exercise station.

John asks if we each want a half cantaloupe or coffee. We decline both.

The conversation begins immediately as Jackie asks, *Where did you find me?* I know she has visited this house before and has asked the same question. John is patient.

Right here. John indicates the floor next to the couch where I am sitting, near the kitchen floor.

Where was my head?

John responds, *I saw your shoes and legs when I came around the corner.*

Jackie stands and looks at the space where she was lying. She returns to the couch.

Could I talk?

No. I would say you were in a very small conscious state; so little. You didn't respond except to a hand squeeze, John replies. *I said,* If you can hear me, squeeze my hand. *We were waiting for help. I asked you again and again if you could hear me.*

Did I move around?, Jackie asks.

No, well, I think you did before I saw you. Because I think you had rolled over on your back.

Jackie stands again and walks to the place where she lay on the floor after the accident. John continues his explanation, addressing me.

I didn't know she was shot. You don't assume that. I didn't think about the car being gone. I suppose if you were in Chicago, but not here. I was thinking, was there an accident? Did Jackie fall? One eye was bulged out, like black already.

He turns back to Jackie. *But your glasses were on. I figured you had fallen and hit the table. Your eye was swollen out to the lens. Very very swollen.*

Later when detectives and cops were here they told me you were shot. It was shocking. All of a sudden there was another party to this. An accident is better than something done on purpose.

John's story returns to the minutes before the shooting. *Me and my son – I had sent Jackie up town to get hot dog buns or something – I told my son we had to go out and cut some boughs. He ate fast and off we go.*

This was really strange. We were up on the hill and my friends, Jim and Devy stopped to look at a Christmas tree. There was this cat that I had seen off and on for several weeks. It was a wild one – no Here kitty, Here kitty *and it would come. It would linger around but keep its distance. All of a sudden that cat was 5 feet away and jumped on Jim. Jim had to pull it off.* John demonstrates by putting his hands to the front of his right shoulder and pretending to wrench a clinging cat away from his coat. *I wonder if that cat heard the bullet.*

Fifteen minutes later we came back to the house. It was a lousy day – November 4 – atrociously cold for that time of year.

When we saw Jackie, we immediately flagged Devy from the road. She is a nurse. She told Jim, I don't think Jackie is going to make it. Of course that is what they said at Reedsburg Hospital and at University Hospital too.

John pauses in his story. He has told Jackie this same story before but is repeating it in answer to her questions and for the record.

Jackie fills the silence. *It is so hard for me to believe that it happened. Did you have blood spots?*

A little. John holds his hands up in a circle smaller than a dinner plate.

Blood was coming down your neck, from when you were face down.

Jackie begins to reenact the crime. She walks to the kitchen, still visible to us in the living room in this unpretentious house. *They stood by your island. I was on the ground. I think I was lying on my stomach. They had told me to hold my arms behind my back.* Jackie stands with her arms behind her back. *It is so unbelievable. They had to bring me in from the garage and they made me lie down and Craig got a pillow from your bed, I think.*

John nods, *Yep.* He and family members and the police and the detectives and the news media have been through the story a hundred times.

The crime reenactment continues as Jackie adds, *And Craig comes out and puts it over my head and shoots. The boys came in the garage door. First they walked past your driveway and kept going but then came back here.*

Two and a half miles from town, John interjects. *I played it out; what if someone would have been up and answered the door? Would the boys have just asked for a ride? You wonder, you wonder. If it had been fifteen minutes sooner they would have had my son here – or all three of us. They might have been steered off. They might have thought differently. Or maybe they were feeling they were caught; thinking what are we going to do?*

I ask John how he has been changed by this experience.

To this day, I pull my keys from my car or truck. I've lost much trust of others! I'm a bit more cautious how I interact with other people. One doesn't know if a person might be carrying a weapon. Now I'm more aware that some humans just don't care who they hurt. For some time, I was very leery answering doors. I would look over my shoulder while watching television. At times I would sense a sort of presence and look to the spot I found Jackie. Sort of haunting; a negative history.

To this day, if Patty or a friend is late, my first thoughts are, Has something gone very wrong? *The innocent world now is seen much more brutal, as has been demonstrated. If people would take the time to be a bit more considerate and respectful of others one wonders how many of these acts would go undone. Little acts of kindness go a long way. Every summer I share some of my garden treats. My mailman enjoys stopping at my mailbox; not to pick up or deliver mail, but to grasp the garden goodies I leave for him.*

Jackie stands and interjects, *Touch.*

John touches the medical pump implanted in her abdomen.

That is under your skin? You had pain.

I had pain in my legs. It is gone 100%.

John turns to Patty who is sitting silently, listening. *For a while Jackie had pain on the whole side of her. Like needles.*

It is evident Jackie wants to change the subject. John is sensitive to this. He continues with his perceptive emotional-hand-holding.

He asks Jackie, *How do you stay fit?*

Walk, walk, walk.

You get your cardio vascular going?

I used to walk for 4 to 6 miles a day.

Holy moly!

I can't walk it now. I walk about 2 miles.

And then do you eat a vegetarian-type diet?

Are you kidding?

So you eat hamburgers and cheese and French fries?

On fries, I will take it easy, Jackie smiles. *But I eat one to two meals a day.*

Jackie glides into her presentation speech. She is standing on the spot where she once lay in a circle of blood. *So many kids think that you are hurt and then you will be normal. But I will be this way until I die.*

The story continues. John and Patty listen attentively, asking questions, as Jackie's audiences always do.

Then John begins to talk about the press of the news media after the accident. *The first couple of weeks, newspaper and TV people were out here on the road. Some would drive up into my fields. They were ringing my doorbell. I didn't want any part of it. I just told them I don't want to discuss anything with you guys. After a week or so, I thought I could do something that would be advantageous; I'd donate a Christmas tree in honor of Jackie. I had a Catholic priest bless the tree and we put it in the local bank. We generated some funds. An interview was held here some weeks later – that was a cold winter – but that day it warmed up and got sunny. It was a nice ceremony. Several local papers and the three TV stations were up here. Some of those guys aren't the same in real life. Some were just the same – nice on TV and nice here. A couple were sure sold on themselves!*

How did the local people react?, I think aloud.

The general response was the same as what Jackie mentioned – the tendency was to hate and have a vindictive attitude. There was shock that this could happen in a little town. It is a shame that someone will hurt a person and then jeopardize themselves for the rest of their lives. They have become a burden on the taxpayers when they could have been productive citizens growing up and doing good.

The local neighbors were not afraid. No fear. I know Craig's family; the shooter's family. They are a bunch of rough riders but you can trust them. Craig and them lived in a mobile home on the east side of town just below the golf course. Josh lived fourteen miles west in Wonewoc; he was relatively poor as well.

I ask John to talk more about the *negative history* he mentioned earlier when speaking about his reactions to Jackie's accident.

It is kind of weird. Every time you take a picture, you get a negative. My mind started going – I'm not a very religious person – but there is something out there responsible for all of this. He can run it fast forward or run it back. It is like it is recorded and He can run the negative back. It happened right here. I walked by the place. An evil act occurred. It isn't a bad spirit but an evil act was created here. I would watch TV here in my living room and all of a sudden I'd look over my shoulder. *You are reminded. It shook you. Is somebody there that is going to shoot you now? It instills a certain fear. You live with it and it becomes the norm. Even today there is a little bit. You learn to have eyes behind your head and your hearing gets better. It is an adaptation. It is stressful. Like another sense was kicking in. The crime was unwarranted. It was there. Sometimes I would pull in the garage at night and wonder if some thug was around the corner. At the gas station, I was thinking that this could be a good place to attack someone.*

John goes on, *Your mind goes wild. It makes you start thinking more. My boy did not want to live in this house for several months (part of it was he stayed with a friend with a pool table). That first night, I said to myself, This is where I live and I came back home. I have to get back on the horse. But it was like…well, dirty. Your living space is dirty. This evil act was done here.*

I've gotten to be – when you see what has happened to Jackie – you learn to treasure every day. I think as I'm lifting weights, how fortunate I am. As my workout gets stressful I often think that Jackie would love to do this.

Adding to the conversation, Jackie says, *I do push ups. My right side doesn't feel so I push up with the left arm. And I try not to fall on my right side. I do 15 of them. You would think I had done 200.*

John follows Jackie's lead and asks, *Do they give you an x-ray every year?*

Every nine months to a year.

And everything is staying the same. [John is referring to the bullet fragments in Jackie's brain and brainstem.]

They are glad everything is staying where it was.

Does this interfere with blood pressure or is everything normal?

It is low – it is about 90 over 60 or 70. It is because I am so even keel.

Was your blood pressure always low? You always were pretty mellow.

I wondered, my audiences are so good. They are quiet. I at first thought it was that I was legally blind; my right side is paralyzed. But it is because I am so mellow.

Did you tell me you are on an antidepressant?

No. Anti-seizure.

That is like a downer? Like it puts you to sleep?

No, it is for the seizures. It makes me so that I don't have them.

You still get a seizure now and then? How often?

About once or twice a week.

How long does it last?

5 seconds to 20 minutes.

When you have one do you have to sit down?

It depends. If I have a grand mal…it is so intense.

I knew a guy who would stand there and just freeze like a statue.

I've had seizures like that. They feel like a video freeze-frame; everything stops in place.

The conversation continues, faster now. The questions and answers between Jackie and John are staccato, like popcorn popping.

Have you had them while you are walking? Yes. That can be dangerous. I think it is fine. If I freeze up, I freeze up. Couldn't you collapse and fall? Yes. If I know … I usually have about 5 seconds when I know I'll have a grand mal seizure. For that, I lay down on the ground. How often a grand mal? That is rare. If I had a grand mal while walking across University Avenue, that would not be good… with the drivers…oh man. But if I have a mini-seizure, I stand very still. Can you hear? No. You can't see anyone. You don't hear anyone. So you don't get a grand mal much on this medication. I thought, wouldn't it be nice if I could take less of my medication. I did and had a grand mal seizure. You have to take this every day? 400 mg in morning and 400 mg at night. Good Lord! That was all brought on too by the shooting? Yes. Wow.

Jackie continues to stand on the carpet where blood once ran out of the back of her head. She talks with John, gesturing intently and making her points. I can see what their long relationship of friendly disagreements and talks has been like. It is being re-created in this space and time. Jackie is able to hold her own. Once again, as I have thought repeatedly in these months of interviews, I reflect on how intelligent Jackie is; how insightful. The ping-pong conversation continues.

I think that I won't ever remember the shooting. It is something that is gone from me. I want to remember it and I don't want to remember it. If I could remember it without feeling it, it would be OK. But I cannot. Once I got hypnotized to remember. I woke up that night sobbing – crying so bad – but then I couldn't remember why I was crying.

Yeah, that's what you've told me. Well, it is probably a good thing that you cannot remember.

Jackie and I walk back through the kitchen to the garage. We are each given two perfectly ripe cantaloupes. I can smell them in the car as we drive back toward Reedsburg. Along the road there is a mailbox shaped like a large lure, with mock hooks on the bottom. Near one house is a sign that reads, *Big Sale. Guns.* The "s" on guns is intentionally written backwards to draw attention, I assume.

Jackie reflects, *This is about the fourth time I've been in that house since the shooting. I get this feeling when I walk into the living room. I can't shake it. It is so sad, 'cause it affected everyone: John, the boys, the community, Craig and Josh – everyone.*

As we drive along, I am looking for garages with open doors or cars that might have the keys left in them. We drive into town again. A sign proclaims, *Welcome to Reedsburg: A Public Power Community since…*I cannot read quickly enough to get all of the words.

And Jackie says, *I love the boys. Most people don't understand…*

SAUK COUNTY SHERIFF'S DEPARTMENT · BUTCH

A....22 caliber slug [travels]...at more than 1000 feet per second.

— Steven Walters, *A Victory Over Violence*,
Journal Sentinel Newspaper, Sunday, March 21, 1999

Butch, County Sheriff.

Jackie and I arrive early for our 10am meeting at the Sauk Prairie Police Department but Butch, the retired Sauk County Sheriff, is already there chatting with the people on duty.

He asks Jackie if he is going to get his hug. She readily agrees.

We move into a vacant office with a chair, desk and two visitor's chairs. Jackie and I sit and Butch pulls the desk chair around to join us in an informal circle. His plaid jacket covers a shirt advertising the value of Outdoor Life. His policeman's hands are easily folded in front of him; two wedding bands on his left hand. His eyes are blue and warm. His white hair and weathered hands alone reveal his seventy-five years.

He has brought us a briefcase full of information about Jackie's case and pulls out the documents one by one. *I have a basement full of this kind of information. This is a special news release. This is a taped interview from one of the witnesses. You hit the mother lode here, Jackie. This is another statement from a sergeant. Oops, this is a secret note.* He takes a note off a packet of papers and sticks it to his forehead.

How am I doing Jackie?

You're doing good.

Butch continues his monologue as he pulls out papers; *This is an interview with John. The only thing I don't have is...when they burned Jackie's car...they burned it over at Junction Road and Golf Course Road and then they ran through the briars toward Reedsburg. They stole the car and then they drove it to Mauston and whipped into McDonalds and ate whatever it is you eat at McDonalds. They stopped and bought gas. They were in Juneau County and then back to Sauk County. And then they torched the car.*

As you go through those pictures, I'll have the girls make copies if you want…you see they still like me up there.

Jackie interjects, *I owe you my life.*

Butch squirms and addresses us both, *I don't think I saved Jackie's life. I assisted with the investigation and directed the inquiry. I have to give credit to the Reedsburg Ambulance that took her to the Reedsburg Medical Center. Those medical people are the ones who saved this miracle lady sitting over here, which I truly think she is. I'm proud that I've known her in my lifetime. In fact we were dealing with the shooting as a murder. How many people get shot in the back of the head and survive? If they had used the .44, we would have said sayonara.*

I'm glad the investigation went the way it did and I'm glad of the outcome and the speed of which we got this corralled. Turning to Jackie, Butch adds, *We feel your case was part of the family and as far as I'm concerned you are still part of the family.*

I think by the time I got to John's house the ambulance was gone. I remember going into the house. You caught old Butchie at the wrong time; I was at home when the officer called me. I always told the officers, I don't want to go to coffee the next morning and hear about a shooting. So I got calls day and night.

We kind of pride ourselves on the law enforcement in Sauk County and couldn't believe that something like this could happen. I don't think that this was a planned assassination on her life. I think they were going to steal a car. Jackie surprised them and I don't think the boys really knew what was the next thing they should do. In their statements, they didn't know what the hell gun they were going to use. I think the pillow was something they saw on a James Bond movie. I don't know what is wrong with society today. I think they see too much on TV. I never learned anything off of TV where I could say that is just like Sauk County law enforcement.

I brag about it, I've had 41 years of law enforcement and never had a fight. I never drew my gun. I have a big mouth and talked my way out of it. You know everybody in Sauk County, *my grandsons say. I always figured if these people were from Sauk County, I wanted to know them. I think it paid off. People come up to me today and know me. I'm sure I talked to them once but don't know who they are now. It doesn't matter; I talk to them. It is a good feeling.*

Craig is at Stanley and Josh is at Red Granite – medium security prisons. Jackie asks. *Do you think the boys got the right sentences?*

I don't know. They've got a long time and I probably won't be around to see if they've learned a lesson or not. If I made the arrest, I always felt I had done my job.

I ask Butch if he was changed in any way by Jackie's case.

People ask me about that and I think that each case affects you in some way. People ask me how I can be so hard. I've seen so much; it is hard for me to show the emotions. I don't let them out; I don't know if that is good or bad. Maybe it will kill me sometime. I do have emotions; I have to deal with the families afterwards. Every case – and Jackie's case was another one – I don't go sit in the coffee shop and spread this around. I keep things in. I sit with this coffee clutch every morning and we solve everything in the world. But nothing is ever talked about shop. I keep it in me because I don't think it is everyone's business.

Butch slowly leans over toward me, smiles, and puts his hand warmly on the arm of my chair. *Now you tell me, Sweetie, what else do you want to know?*

Jackie and I thank Butch for his stories and the many documents he has given us.

EXCERPTS
FROM POLICE REPORTS, INTERVIEWS AND NARRATIVES ON JACKIE'S CASE

Dispatch Report, November 4, 1995

Dispatcher: 9-1-1

Caller: Um, yes. Someone I think broke into our house. Our doors unlocked, or no, no one did break in but uh they lay, er my dad's uh friend is laying down there, her, she's bloody and everything…

Dispatcher: OK what happened?

Caller: I don't know. We were up on the hill, we came down, her car is gone...

Dispatcher: Is the guy breathing?

Caller: No it's a lady.

Dispatcher: Is she breathing?

Caller: We need an ambulance I mean I think she is. Dad, is she breathing? Yeah but, she's having a seizure or something.

Dispatcher: OK. If anything changes give us a call back OK?

Caller: All right bye.

Dispatcher: Something's weird...

• • •

A few minutes later,

Dispatcher: Hi this is the Sheriff's Department calling.

Answerer: Yes.

Dispatcher: How's the lady doing?

Answerer: I think she's having a seizure. I, I don't, she's laying here and I was holding her hand and she had fallen see and I, I don't know, I mean...

Dispatcher: OK is she alert and conscious?

Answerer: She, well she, she's deler, kind of delirious.

Dispatcher: She's bloody because she fell then correct?

Answerer: I think so but it looks as though she might, yeah I think primarily yeah.

Dispatcher: OK because when the first call came in they didn't know if somebody was there or hurt her or what?

Answerer: No there's no one in the house. We came here but she had her car here but I don't know where the car is which is really strange.

Dispatcher: OK well we're sending a detect er a deputy over also.

Answerer: OK.

Dispatcher: But an ambulance has been paged um, I just want to make that she's OK. That's she's breathing OK?

Answerer: She's breathing yeah but it's just like she's semi-conscious...

Dispatcher: OK well the ambulance has been paged, they'll be there shortly and uh a deputy should be there real short OK?

Answerer: OK. Bye.

• • •

From Officer Mike's notes on the incident

Officer Mike:...*I then went in to the residence and, in the living room, laying in a supine position, I observed a female subject who appeared to have some serious head injuries. At this time, I radioed to the Reedsburg Ambulance that it was an extreme emergency.*

• • •

From Officer Kevin's notes on the incident

Officer Kevin: *I noted that there were two spots on the carpet, approximately four feet into the living room area, that appeared to be blood. I also noted at that point that the furniture was in unnatural positions, noting that it was pushed into the center of the living room, away from the walls...John said he moved the furniture at Devy's [the nurse] request. At the time he found [Jackie], she was lying tight to the end of the sofa with her head...*

Officer Kevin: *On arrival at the scene, I explained...that some information was that two male individuals had been seen walking CTH V, and at this point two males had been seen leaving the car which had been set afire south of Reedsburg off of South Dewey. I told him that at this point we did not have a good description of these and asked that he initially start with a...canvass...*[Many people reported seeing]*...two younger boys walking north on CTH V on the right side of the road...stated that the taller one had a shaved head...the smaller person looked like he was carrying a duffle bag or something small like that, like a suitcase or something under his arm.*

• • •

From Officer Tom's notes on the incident

Officer Tom: *Once back at the office, I did receive telephone calls from Nurse Ben...of the UW Trauma Center...The hospital personnel were concerned about what they were considering a Jane Doe with a gunshot wound and not having much information to go on. They wanted to know if there was anything we needed as far as evidence collection and security measures...*[We asked them] *to collect any clothing that was being worn by Ms. Millar at the time of her treatment and also to collect blood for us. Nurse...stated that that he had also noted that there was some bruising on the shoulders on Ms. Millar as through she had been grabbed very hard from behind. He also said that she possibly had a torn bladder or urinary problem, probably caused by some type of blunt trauma...*

• • •

From Detective Mary's notes on the incident

Detective Mary: *On 12-4-95 I made telephone contact with Dr. Allen..., University Hospital, Madison... He advised me that he is the treating physician for Jackie Millar. We discussed Millar's present condition. [He] stated that Jackie Millar would survive. That she had Severe Neurological Damage from the bullet wound to her head.*

I discussed with him the statute definition of great bodily harm. He stated that the statute would fit Jackie Millar's condition. That she presented with a substantial risk of death. That she has a impairment of her neurological system.

ABILITY AND DISABILITY

＊＞＜＠

As we last parted, Jackie told me that she had considered
stopping our conversations for a month or so.

The funny stories are great and I truly enjoy them, she said.
But the sad stories make my chest tighten and I feel badly later.
But, after thinking about this,
I decided to maintain our same interview pace.

＊＞＜＠

And so we continue. Jackie talks about her altered abilities and her disabilities.

When things were rough or when I was so, so tired, I consciously went to the fields.
They existed in my mind and went on forever. That was my sanctuary. They were
so peaceful. The grass was glowing green and there were wildflowers everywhere. The
trees were mammoth. There was a lake, so blue, and a matching sky. I could smell
everything. I was in oneness with it all. I was alone. And I could walk normally.

I don't remember anything from when I was hurt.

I remember waking up. My head hurt. I had a brain infection but knew it hurt
less if I lay on my side, so I struggled to do that. I was like a child. I couldn't tell
anyone what was happening; I had no control. It has been said that I died on
November 4, 1995. But I became alive again. The doctors compared me to a two-
year-old and I had to relearn everything.

I would open my eyes and look around. I didn't say, Hi, *but I looked at the space*
in the ways a baby views her world. After about six weeks in the hospital I was able
to recognize my sons and mouthed words to them. I said, I love you.

Jackie is moving slowly this day as she talks about the physical changes in her
life. Serendipitously we have chosen a day to meet when her focus on her disabilities outweighs her more customary pride in her abilities.

It is harder for me today because when I got the pump in my abdomen for the mus-
cle relaxant; they set it at 50 mg. Then they upped it to 100 mg. That was great.
I could walk halfway normal. I could walk fast; my right hand would lay flat. I

was in seventh heaven. Now my neurologist bumped it up to 125 and it is like I'm in a fog. My right leg is mush. That's why I've got the brace on it now. It will have a certain amount of time for it to get over the 125, but there is a saying, for every little bit of heaven there is some hell and I second that.

Since our conversation topic is on physical abilities and I have heard that the optic nerve behind Jackie's right eye was severed by the bullet, I ask, *What do you see, Jackie?*

I think I can see bright yellow, red, green, and gray. I see colors. But my eyes are very, very cloudy. How much do I see? About — this is just a guess — about 3/10 of what is actually there. I don't see detail. I don't see my sons; I wish I would see their faces. Their faces are blank. Your face is blank. It is amazing. Kids — my audience — they come up to me and say, Remember me, I am the one that felt your head. *I don't remember them. I wish I did. I see very poorly at night. That is why when I come into a room I will put on the lights. My two sons, I think they forget that, whether knowingly they forget or whether unknowingly they forget. They will have pictures that they want me to see and I see them. We pretend.*

I say I can read email but I cannot tell you the letters because I don't see them. The letter 'e,' for example, I may see only the bar across the letter. I have gotten very very good at telling the letters. But there are times, and this will depend on whether the letters are small, that I see only half of...I will read every other line. I am great at getting the gist of something. When I have difficulty, I will take my finger down and read where my finger is. I've learned many little tricks.

I am excellent at spelling. I don't know why. I just know how to spell. It's hard to put your finger on it.

I look out this window. There are trees. I cannot see the birds. I can see a little bit of movement from the wind. If a cardinal came and sat on the railing, I would see a red blob; and I would tell somebody, I see a red cardinal *and they would be abuzz thinking I really saw a red cardinal. But I see only a red blob and I assume it is a cardinal.*

So you are translating, I reply and Jackie nods.

I have to be careful. I went to the Art Fair on the Square with my aide and her friend. They were looking at a piece of art and I went ahead and I turned and I thought I saw her. I thought for sure it was her and this person walked up and walked past me and it wasn't her. Part of me was ashamed. Part of me felt sad. I rely – this is dumb – I rely on seeing. That is strange coming from a legally blind woman. But I wasn't born this way. I was born normal *and I only came by it ten -and-a-half years ago. I want to think that I am a seeing person. When you are so sure of something and then it isn't true… I know I'm not perfect. I know it. But I feel that I should have known the woman wasn't my aide.*

Jackie stands and walks to the sliding glass door in her apartment as she often does while we talk. She pauses, returns to her dark green recliner and picks a piece of white lint off the seat before sitting down.

I remark, *Jackie, you just leaned over and picked up a piece of white lint off of your chair. How did you see that?*

She sits and replies. *If I look at the speck from here, I don't see it. It is about knowing what the speck is and finding it. I think I remember from before my accident. If I get a Diet Coke from the refrigerator, I don't know how I see it. This will sound funny. I pray to God that I find what I'm looking for and I get it. I think that is how I do a lot of things.*

Up there, Jackie gestures toward her bookcase, *I've got a lot of pictures. From sitting here and looking I will tell you I know who is in the shots. I don't have good memory but I can tell you.* Jackie stands and walks to the bookcase, gesturing from one framed picture to the next. *That is a picture of Chad, this is a picture of Chad and Lisa, that is a picture of me, that is a picture of Derek and Ann. Maybe it is because those pictures are always there and maybe I remember them.*

Jackie stops and takes off her leg brace, dropping it heavily on the floor next to her green chair.

What do you hear, Jackie?

There is minimal damage. I have buzzing in my ear.

Teasingly I say, *That's the lawnmower outside!*

The gun was loud and that created damage, Jackie replies with a polite laugh at my attempt to lighten the conversation.

Tell me about your right side, I continue.

There was pain. It is hydro – something or other – it is super, to the 100th degree, I feel it. They have deadened the muscle in my whole right side. They had to make the muscles so the muscles wouldn't constrict. My right side is off. It is like this leg, Jackie taps her right leg, *is always trying to catch up; it lags behind. I am sorry it is behind but,* Jackie smiles and pauses for effect, *I am alive.*

From the bottom of my foot to the top of my head it is different on the right side of me. I will eat something and I will slobber. I will have something drip down from the right side of my face. When my son would eat with me, he would always tell when I needed to wipe my face. I wouldn't know that I had gotten a piece of food on this side. But he would tell me. My friends and family would tell me. I don't feel anything on the right side. The right side of my face wants to sag so I do exercises with my mouth wide open to make me look as normal as possible. I have no feeling on my skin but there is pain inside my leg and arm.

I am getting so that I will take things with my right hand; I will try to take it. I know that I can't carry things with my right hand. I've gotten very good at using my left. My right hand feels all prickly. It feels like a thousand pricklers are in it. Like my hand is asleep but only ten times more. My fingers want to curl up; they feel more natural when flat. I think I have to keep them straight. I think that it would give me the ability to walk straight, if I could walk straight-handed.

Jackie shakes her head and says, *Oh, jeez. I know that my request is very amateurish. It isn't solving a miracle. It isn't diagnosing a cure for cancer. It is just that, walking straight-handed...* Jackie is silent.

I compliment her on her frankness and ask how she is able to talk about all of this so openly.

It is weird. I think I have wondered that myself. Why am I not angry at Craig and Josh? I am not angry at them. I wish that they hadn't shot me in the head, that they hadn't shot me. But you know you can't be vindictive. You can't be sorry, because I would end up in a small padded room at Mendota [Mental Health Hospital].

More silence as Jackie pauses and finally ends our day's conversation with, *But sometimes I just want to get back Jackie.*

UNIVERSITY OF WISCONSIN HOSPITAL AND CLINICS REHABILITATION

It snowed last night. I remember the gardener planting burnt orange marigolds and hot pink petunias in the circular bed in front of Jackie's apartment when we began our journey through her story. Today we are headed to the University of Wisconsin Rehabilitation Clinic to revisit the place where Jackie lived for three months following the accident; to see the rooms where she went through rehabilitation and recovery.

I ask about the pain in her leg. *OK,* she replies. *But yesterday,* she confides, *I lost total sight in my right eye. And then I had double vision in my left eye. It went on for forty-five minutes.*

I ask Jackie if she felt frightened. *Yes. It was very frightening. That hadn't ever happened before.*

We park and walk into this huge teaching hospital through twinkling snowflakes and other non-denominational holiday decorations. A very elderly volunteer greets us. Jackie asks her how we get to the rehabilitation unit and although she means to help us, she cannot hear Jackie well in the noisy area. Jackie persists, explaining her brain injury, and the message is finally conveyed when the woman realizes Jackie does not have an appointment, but has simply come to revisit old haunts.

We are directed toward 4BW – Fourth Floor, B wing, West. After talking with two other people with identification badges along the way, we arrive at *the hospital within a hospital.* Admission is limited by a door with a sign explaining that the air we are about to breathe is Hepa Filtered. We walk in.

I see several people moving in wheelchairs down the long hallway. We walk to the nurse's station to explain our visit when one of the women says, *Jackie?!! I was your occupational therapist and worked with you in learning services!*

They catch up on eleven years of history quickly talking about Jackie's sons, her speaking engagements, and then her physical abilities.

Word has spread through the floor that Jackie is there and another woman comes up to us. *I'm Anne and I was one of your nurses. I had you come and speak to the rehabilitation nurses. Can I hug you?*

Jackie's answer isn't a surprise as the two women hug.

I am indebted to you. I can talk. I can walk, although I can't run, Jackie says, gleaming.

Did your vision resolve at all?

I can see your hair. I can see that you are wearing something red. I can't see your face.

The conversation continues but it becomes clear people have work to do. We ask what we may visit and are told we may tour the occupational therapy day room, the shower room (which now has a whirlpool tub), the gym, and the visitor area near the heliport. We decide to walk first to the visitor's area where we can look out on the helicopter landing area.

This is the old heliport, a woman sitting near the window tells us. That means this would have been where Jackie was brought by Medivac after her accident. Jackie stands by the picture window looking out at the yellow circles on the pavement below.

It is all so, so…it is all hidden in my brain. I was totally unconscious when the helicopter brought me to this place.

There is quiet as Jackie looks out the window. I notice she is not wearing her red shoes this day.

I had – what do you call it – I wasn't able to go to the bathroom like normal people.

A catheter?, I suggest.

Yes. I kept pulling it out. The last time I did that the nurses said, OK, let's see if she can do it by herself. I did. Oh, yes. I didn't want the catheter put back in.

It is interesting what memories come back for you when we go to places that were significant in your accident and recovery.

Jackie agrees, *Like you have said, I remember things if they had an emotional effect on me or my sons.*

I remember that one time, in January, they let me go home for a few hours…

The story is interrupted by a man's voice.

Brian…here, he says.

Jackie does not remember him but he good-naturedly explains.

I was your psychologist. The place is very different now, so you wouldn't remember it. When you were here there was no wallpaper and nothing on the floors. Everything was painted.

Looking at me, Brian inquires, *Who is this?*

I reach out to shake hands and tell him my name. Jackie explains our project, telling him that we are writing a book that isn't mean or cruel. We are capturing the positive elements of the story.

Jackie continues, addressing Brian, *You didn't give up on me, even though I wanted to give up. Now I see from my heart; that is my eyes.*

Brian smiles warmly and Jackie jumps immediately to her burning questions about her memory. *Did I remember anything when you talked with me?*

Brian pauses and asks, *May I talk about your case in front of Judy?*

Yes.

We talked about whether you actually remembered things or if you remembered what people told you about events.

It makes me mad that I can't remember.

It is unlikely you will remember anything from that whole period. People with brain injuries sometimes remember their rehabilitation but the memories are vague. I remember that you were fiercely independent, highly motivated, and angry or puzzled over how this could have happened to you. Anyone would be puzzled over such a thing. Listening to your voice now I hear a more halting quality now than before. You have adopted a pattern of speech and pacing that allows you to remember words well. You are very clear and coherent.

I speak to groups. I try to be as clear as possible so I can say all the words I want. Jackie moves on, changing the topic, as she sees Brian glance at his watch. Her ability to read body language continually surprises me. She cannot see perfectly but she reads people's every subtle movement. Brian notices and says, *I have a meeting in two minutes but it has been great to see you, Jackie.*

The people here are top notch.

You brought it out of us.

A kind exchange. Heartfelt. People do remember Jackie. I expect they see things with their trained eyes that I don't.[5]

Brian heads off to his meeting and Jackie and I walk toward the physical therapy day room.

Being here does bring back memories. They are good memories. The nurses, when they had me, I was – I think – a handful. They would put me in a wheelchair and let me loose. I remember that I would go around and around in a small circle because I couldn't use my right hand and leg. That was good because they knew where I was. They gave me a wheelchair where I had to stretch my legs. I got so I was pretty good. But I knew I had limitations on how far I could go.

As we start to enter the day room, we are gently turned away. I see a woman

---

[5] These professionals know Jackie was shot in the back of her head with a star-tipped, hollow-point bullet. They understand the anatomy of a person's brain and know the bullet fragments likely tore through her cerebellum, the part of the brain that links sensory perception and motor functions that allow muscles to glide, fine-tuned. The cerebellum is also home to cognitive functions like processing language, paying attention, and appreciating music. The bullet fragments also likely cut into the limbic area of Jackie's brain where memory, motivation, decision-making and emotion are both stored and connected. The staff knows she is hemiplegic, which means she has permanently lost much muscle function on one side of her body – in Jackie's case, her right side.

with a brain injury working with her physical therapist. Much about the woman's appearance tells me *motorcycle accident.*

We make our way to the rehabilitation gym back on the second floor, again with help from staff wearing badges. No one is in the gym so we walk among the exercise machines. Some of them are the typical devices seen in health clubs and gyms across the U.S. Others are more specialized like the half car with functional doors and seatbelts. Jackie walks to the silver rail on a stationary walkway and touches the cool metal with her left hand.

This contraption, she says. *The nurses and occupational therapists and physical therapists were great. I don't remember learning how to sit again, but do remember learning to stand and walk. A big belt went around me so the therapists could hold me. There were stanchions – like this – with rails on two sides. Of course, there was no need for two rails because my right side would not work. I was wheeled over to the stanchions and told to stand up.* You're nuts, I can't do it, *I said to the occupational therapist.* You can, *she replied. This was a torture machine.*

I would tell my brain to make my legs work. I'd sit in the wheelchair and look at the stanchions and pretty soon I could stand up and then I took one step and I cried because, Oh boy, I could do it. *Constantly, constantly, constantly, I stood and finally took that first step. You'd have thought I'd run a marathon. I went to physical therapy Monday through Friday, in the morning and again in the afternoon. I can remember! I can remember!*

Jackie pauses and remembers a post-accident incident. *When Craig got up to the witness stand at his sentencing hearing, they asked him what he had done. I did not want to hear it again. I tried to leave quietly. But when I was in the court room, my foot wouldn't do what I wanted it to do and so I talked to it. I went out in the hallway and I walked up and down, up and down. I had a sheriff's department man who walked it with me. He was being my bodyguard that day. I told my foot to straighten out and then we would walk straight. It would turn over on its side. It always acts up at the most inopportune times.*

Jackie returns to the present, *They had the speech – the language pathologist – come in afternoons and she would work on me. She would say a word and she would want me to say a word. It was one word at a time. She would say four words, I would remember one word. At 3:30 I remember I would rest and sleep. I didn't like to work on speech. It wasn't the pathologist; it was I thought I didn't need it. And it wasn't until they played back a tape recording of me talking that I realized.*

On the tape for the sentencing hearing, your voice is much different than it is now, I add.

That was funny, I would speak and say Jac – kie *rather than Jackie. They had to do a lot of fixing up to play that tape. A lot. I don't talk the way I used to talk before the accident, but I don't talk the same as what I used to after the accident.*

In her presentations, Jackie tells listeners that as part of her rehabilitation she *even* had to learn how to go to the bathroom again. I ask, *How did they teach you how to go to the bathroom?*

That was cute. I don't like talking about it. I wore diapers. I had to have diapers on while they taught me how to go to the bathroom. They would take me in and sit me down on the toilet. That was… I would be afraid I'd fall. But they had me sit until I went to the bathroom. And slowly it triggered something in me to not go to the bathroom unless I was sitting on a toilet. You talk about demoralizing things…but it was just something I had to learn. I didn't like to learn…I thought I already knew everything. Jackie laughs. *I thought – this is hard to say now – but I thought that the hospital was my home. I got the chance to go home for a few hours in January and that was new to me. It was April 15 when I was ready to go home. I was ready for the condo – I remember that date.*

When I went home from rehab, I had an aide, bless her heart. Her name is Barb and she is my support broker now. She had been told by the hospital to do this and that. She knew I wasn't going to follow their instructions. I got along pretty well by not following their directions. I think I don't listen to, Be safe; you do it our way and we are being safe for you. *I look at it and I say,* No, I take chances. This is the new Jackie. *I look at my life. I don't…I have seven bullet fragments inside my head – five in my brain, one in my brain-stem and one in my left eye socket. They could move at the drop of a hat. I wear glasses to protect my eye from a blow. I've got a limited amount of time. I'm going to get the most I can. I'm going to get the most I can.*

Silence as Jackie looks around the empty rehabilitation gym again and then she says, *I should have been angry. I should have questioned why. But my brain needed time. It was watching out for me when I was here. It was saying,* She can't handle it right now.

Her eyes rest on a vinyl-covered table. *I must have been on that flat surface because they massaged me. They had to massage my legs because I had been asleep for six weeks.*

Jackie pauses, considering. *They could have put me in a nursing home but they did not. They believed in me.*

We leave the room and the torture machines behind us. Again we turn the wrong way in the maze of hallways and find a woman to redirect us. As happened repeatedly, she is willing to walk with us until we are headed right. As we walk, Jackie tells her she was a patient here eleven years ago for three months. She tells a bit of her story and the woman listens and then says quietly, *I know your story; I followed it in the newspaper. I am honored to meet you.*

And as we leave the hospital, the aged volunteer at the information desk calls out to Jackie, *How did you do?* Smiling, Jackie replies, *I was at rehab and met a lot of people.*

It is true.

SISTER · PAM

Jackie's younger sister comes to talk with us; Jackie has described her as a salty sailor.

Pam walks into the apartment and fills the kitchen with her forceful, *God, I'm dying. Do you have any Coke?* In colloquial Wisconsin-speak, Coke means pop or soda – something, anything to drink. I hear the rustle of glasses and the refrigerator door swing shut.

From the living room, I still cannot see Pam but larger than life I hear her say to Jackie, *You took TWO Vicodin? Jeez, take one next time.*

Pam enters the room. She is stocky, forceful, slightly disheveled, with a straight-forward handshake. I like her instantly.

Later she tells me she used to be bossy and bull-headed, to which I smile. *I could bully Jack into anything, but she changed and I changed. I looked at my sister and told myself that if she can change, so can I.*

Pam is the one person who can tell us about young Jackie, or Jack, and so I ask.

Remember the horse and the donkey, Jack? A sleepy nod but no real recognition from Jackie who deeply is under the influence of the two Vicodin tablets, taken to ease her pain from yesterday's surgery. *Growing up, I was the rider. Jack was so afraid. Once she forgot that a donkey can kick sideways and lost both her shoes trying to run away from the ornery animal. Jack was a good athlete; she was so fast. Now I keep forgetting that she cannot walk as fast as I can. I smashed her head in the door one day.* Jackie smiles and nods with more energy, perhaps remembering this time.

Pam goes on, *And another day I stopped hearing the tap tap of her white cane behind me. I thought she was teasing me by hiding around the corner. I went back to find her and she told me she was seeing snakes. She knew I was phobic about snakes so I assumed more teasing. But that wasn't the case. It was her first grand mal seizure. The doctors had told us that if she had no seizures for the first year after her accident, she would not have them. The snake incident happened a year and a week later.*

Pam continues, *Jackie was a pro at her work. It was her life: her work and her boys. She could stand before 500 people and talk but once out of her job, she was so quiet and shy. After her divorce from Mark, she decided she wanted a new life and met a bunch of crap-tacular guys.* There is a sleepy, affirmative reply.

Our family has a sick sense of humor. It is a way of coping. I remember when Jackie and I were in a restaurant after the accident. She took a bite of her hamburger. She chewed. She chewed. She chewed. Finally she asked me if my meat was tough. I told her to open her mouth and out fell one of those little paper cups the salsa comes in. We laughed so loudly the man in the next booth looked over and finally said, It isn't nice to laugh at a retarded person. *I tried to explain but he just reamed me out. He thought I was just this monster.*

Jackie smiles lazily and says, *Remember the time you picked me up in front of my apartment? I fell under the truck cab, on the ice. You tried to help me. You fell. We both lay under the cab laughing.*

What happened on the day of the accident, I ask. And why do you call it an accident?

Jackie shifts her weight to her other hip with a grimace and rousts herself to answer the second question. *It is easier to say* accident *than to say that someone set out to deliberately hurt me. Besides, I cannot say the word…it begins with an i…what is the word? I cannot remember. I say accident only because it is easier to remember.*

Incident?

Yeah. Drives me crazy, Pam complains. *It wasn't an accident!*

Pam begins to explain what happened the day of the accident and Jackie shifts again uncomfortably in her chair.

As always, Jackie seems eager to hear the answer to the question about what happened the day of the accident. Every detail, every subtlety, every nuance.

I found out the next morning. Jack was a Jane Doe to the police overnight. My ex-brother-in-law called me. I was just bawling so hard; I couldn't imagine anyone would hurt my sister. With my *mouth, I could see me getting hurt, but not her.*

In the hospital, she looked normal except for her left eye. It bulged out like a ping pong ball. Her right eye and her head, Pam gestures indicating a turban-like wrapping, *were bandaged. I took it all in. I sat down next to her.*

That night I called intensive care ten times. The nurses were so nice to me. I did not work for a month. I sat with Jack, reading, so she could hear my voice.

She developed pneumonia and had a fever of 104 degrees. They kept her room at about 50 degrees to cool her down and I sat there next to her shivering and reading aloud about angels thinking that she was tougher than I had thought.

One of the craziest things was when my husband told me this story. He is a guy who sees the world in black and white. He said he walked into Jackie's room when she was still on the ventilator. She was in the coma but he thought he heard her say, in her own voice, You have to forgive them because I have. *He was shaken by this experience.*

Jack was in an induced coma for four weeks and spent another two weeks waking up. We went through triumphs together. She couldn't swallow but kept pulling out her feeding tubes and finally the therapists decided to teach her to swallow. They worked and worked with her and finally put barium in a blueberry muffin so they could trace it and see if it had gone down her throat. The doctor said she was totally blind, that her pathways were destroyed. I cried more tears. She loved photography and driving her candy apple red Honda. But I knew her eyes were able to follow me around the room and she did end up having some vision.

She re-learned everything. With her right side paralyzed, she couldn't sit up. She would just fall over. As she re-learned some words, she would tell me, I'm sick. I cannot do this. *But she just wanted to get out of doing it. And then after she stood for the first time, we could not hold her back. She told everyone who came into her room that she had permission to go for walks. The staff finally tied her in her wheelchair.*

Jackie raises her head and sleepily interjects, *They tied me in tightly.*

Pam continues, *Jack became a good liar. She wanted to progress faster. You could not talk to her when she was eating. She would whip some food at you if you told her she was eating too fast. After two months she was moved from the University Hospital to the Learning Center. Her pace was remarkable. But ornery... More than once she got no lunch because she refused to make her own food.*

The nurses told me I had to socialize my sister again, so we would go out to restaurants. She would shovel down her food and be done before I had taken a few bites and then she was ready to go. I would get to laughing about something and she would stay with me.

I took her to her home. The nurses said the only thing she couldn't do was to climb the stairs because they had not worked on that yet. So I turned my back for a minute and Jack scooted up the stairs on her butt and locked herself in the bedroom. I called the University Rehabilitation Center staff and they said to bribe her. Offer her food and she will come out. *I got her out with cookies but then she tried to bite me. I called rehab again and they said,* Be firm with her. Tell her that if she tries to bite you again she will have to return to rehab again right now. And mean it. She is stubborn because she is scared. She has been through a lot.

Jackie has been listening to each word and asks if she was really that self-centered.

Yes, you were. For several years. You were so determined to get better. I was with you every step of the way; you don't remember. And lie! You would lie all the time. Do you remember? No? Oh yea, you don't remember all the lying!

I know I went through a lot, Jackie replies, slowly enunciating each word.

And remember when you wanted a job so badly?

Jackie smiles and shakes her head, shrugging. *No.*

You were a mess. You were still so jumpy at any noises. Your head was not together. You could not find the words you wanted; they just came out wrong, all confused. We tried to find a job for you but there was no work. You couldn't type with only one hand and you could not see. Finally I talked with my brother-in-law who worked at Sauk Schools. I told him, My sister has a great story. She can talk with troubled kids.

Remember the time I dyed your hair for you, Jack? You wouldn't get down where I could reach your head. You are taller than I am, you know. The dye was going everywhere! We got to laughing at all the dye.

That's the last time on God's green earth you will ever dye my hair, Jackie frowns. *I went to speak to inmates at Columbia maximum prison the next day. There were twelve of them and I asked them,* What is different about me? *Scottie whispered loudly,* The color of your hair, it is purple. *Oh, my God. What you did! I had to wear a hat for six weeks.*

I offered to dye it a different color, Pam complains, smiling.

No, no, no, you will never touch my hair again!

Jackie pulls herself, painfully, up out of the chair. She walks with her heavy leg. *I have something to tell you. The angels. The bright light.*

There is silence. I listen. Pam listens.

I went out to eat with my aide. We were eating and then we finished. I felt funny, like a seizure was coming on. And then I saw it. A bright light came down from the ceiling and there were angels in it. I knew it wasn't time yet, but the bright light told me that God is going to...He is going to...

Moments pass. Jackie walks in a small circle and then says, *Angels are always with you. They communicate but not by talking. They told me my time is near but that Chad, Pam and Craig will be OK.*

Why Chad, Pam and Craig? I ask thinking *son, sister and shooter.*

Chad because he has always been so sick. Pam because it is just you and me. And Craig? A mystery.

Pam responds, *After this happened, Jackie asked me to talk with Craig because I had to become OK with everything. I went to the prison and I told this story to Craig. He cried. And I ended up feeling sorry for him; I'm still mad at myself for that.*

JACKIE'S SONS · DEREK & CHAD

A central refrain in Jackie's story is this:

My sons! My sons! Jackie says with her head down, a slight smile, and rocking gently side to side. *You can do anything to me but don't hurt my kids.*

Derek, Jackie and Chad Millar

My sons were there with me in the hospital. Jackie remembers vividly. *They were told I had a 2% chance of recovery and that, if I did live, I'd be a vegetable the rest of my life. Each one dealt with this in totally opposite ways. One immersed himself in his college classes and the other went into depression. Their mother was hurt.*

SON · DEREK

Derek lives in mid-Iowa. Like Reedsburg Wisconsin, many Iowa towns feel safe. Doors are often unlocked. Children play freely.

I visit Derek and Ann's home on a September evening. I can hear the noises from the local high school football game spreading out over the whole community along with the glow of the Friday night lights. Derek and I sit at two ends of his living room and I ask him to talk about his experiences in and around his mother's accident.

I was a junior at the University of Wisconsin-Platteville, studying mechanical engineering.

The shooting occurred Saturday, about 5 in afternoon. I had no information until my Dad called me early Sunday morning. I was asleep. I was kind of out of it. The answering machine picked up and I heard Dad telling me to answer the phone. All he would elaborate was that Mom was hurt fairly seriously, but he wouldn't go any further than that on the phone.

He told me to pick up my brother, who was also a student in Platteville and head back to Madison as soon as we could. I could tell by his voice that it was pretty serious. I was nervous especially when he wouldn't elaborate. Nevertheless, I picked Chad up and we headed for Madison. Chad and I aren't always the most talkative people and that morning as we mostly sat in the car for a little over an hour we did not say much. We were just mulling over in our heads what could be going on. I was nervous; I don't know what Chad was thinking.

When we arrived at Mom's condo, my Dad and my Grandma were there. They kind of sat us down. I wish I could remember everything they said. They said she was shot in the head.

What were you feeling as you heard the story, I interrupt.

Shocked, that's the best word I can use. It began to sink in. I had been conjuring up scenarios of what was going on. But I didn't expect what I was being told. It took five or ten minutes to realize that life was going to be a little bit different now. I didn't realize in what ways. I could tell from their reactions that they were pretty upset. My Dad and Grandmother had been living it through the night. They were tired, strung out. Telling us was bringing it all up again for them. I didn't cry. I don't think Chad cried. We didn't have that kind of reaction when we were home.

Mom was in intensive care. Just as I got to the hospital, a bunch of my other family members arrived – mostly from my dad's side. Some of them were crying. My Dad and my Grandma went to the intensive care room with us.

Mom was hooked up to everything. Her hair was shaved. Her eye was swollen shut and purple. It was pretty frightening. She had tubes in her arms. The pressure relief tubes were in her head. She was obviously in a coma; not conscious. That is ironic – just the visual images. I don't remember a lot about that first experience; how long I stayed in the room. I am sure I held her hand. I stayed there quite a while.

It was hard to leave, even to go to my Grandma's. Every time I would visit her in the future, it was awfully hard to leave the hospital. Everyone congregated at my Grandma's house. She was the glue.

The thing I remember most about that Sunday was that I was so exhausted – being woken up early and being so tired. I laid down in Grandma's house in the living room and just collapsed. I don't take naps, but I fell asleep. And then I think that was the time it really hit home. In my dream, for whatever reason, I was remembering all the nice things before the accident. It was almost like the dream I was in was actually the reality and the reality was a dream. When I woke up, for two seconds I felt really good and then I recognized I was in my Grandma's living room and I felt really sad. Then I felt really bad. Instead of waking up from a bad dream and feeling relief, this was the opposite.

I went back to the hospital that night. I stayed through Monday. I did go back to Platteville later on Monday evening. That is part of my personality. Even in extreme situations, I still felt this commitment to school. I was nervous about missing a lot of classes but it was so hard because that isn't where I wanted to be. I was torn but I also knew I could have dropped out or taken a break but my Mom wouldn't have wanted me to do that. She would have yelled at me. That is the way she is now. She gets mad at you if you do things for her even if you have the right intentions. I was in Madison weekends. That was tough. My professors at college were great and really, really supportive. A couple of them really cut me some breaks. I remember one of my engineering professors – there was a fund established for my Mom – one of my professors made a really generous donation. He didn't say anything, but I found out about it. Friends at college were out for my best interest.

I was Mom's Power of Attorney. She was the kind of person who had talked about her death before so ironically I knew what she wanted. If she were in a vegetative state, she would want to end it at that point. But the doctors didn't bring any of that up directly. I remember someone, maybe my dad, asked if I had thought about what you'd do for your Mom if she was in a vegetative state. I didn't want to think about that. I knew what I would do but the question suggested she might not make it.

I don't remember much about school that year other than how generous my professors were. I probably did bury myself in school. With engineering there is enough work to do; I found ways to handle it. I don't know if they were healthy or not but they were a distraction. I don't really drink; I didn't get into that.

We begin to talk about forgiveness and I remember what Jackie has told me about her sons. Neither of them uses Craig and Josh's names when they speak of the boys who committed the crime.

I didn't forgive right away either. I thought I was really over things and then I realized I wasn't. I went to one of the sentences for the one that actually shot her and during that court experience I realized I really hadn't forgiven yet.

My Mom – it comes so easily – I think that is a good thing that she can do it. She visits him in prison. She was really nervous about my and Chad's reactions to that. Her saying she loves him and how I respond to that. If I hadn't forgiven them that would really rub me the wrong way. I think the boy who shot her is genuinely sorry; that is all I want to hear and see. My Mom has to live with it all and that has to be incredibly difficult. She was the leader of forgiveness. She was one of the first people to truly forgive. None of the family members wanted to do that.

And she is human; sometimes she shows her frustration.

I was at the trial; at that sentencing. What I remember about that is that it was very emotional. My Mom had a video[6] and some people spoke about her and her

---

[6] Transcript from Jackie's video taped presentation at the sentencing hearings: I had a job, good interpersonal skills, business skills, and organizational skills. I had an active social life. My family and friends were most important to me. I prided myself on being there for my family and friends. I lived a simple life with simple goals and philosophies. I looked forward to moving to the country and getting married someday and being there to support my grandchildren.

Who am I now? I'd like to believe I am the same person but that isn't true. My deficits range from physical to cognitive to emotional. My vocabulary does not come easily. I can't say what I think. I have to concentrate before I say anything and ask myself if it is the right thing. Sometimes I say just the wrong thing and don't even realize it. Talking on the phone is next to impossible, let along functioning at my job. I had to have assistance preparing this speech and practice to tape it. It would have taken me about twenty minutes before, now it took weeks. I cannot see; everything is blurry. I am legally blind. Because of my blindness I cannot survive in everyday life. I cannot cook or clean or even go out of the house without assistance. It takes me three times as long as it should to vacuum the house. My memory is poor with day to day information. There is a span of time that I do not remember at all. My right side does not function properly. There is pain in my shoulder and leg. My organizational skills are poor. Due to my vision, verbal and cognitive problems, my interpersonal skills suffer at best. My family and *life. I wasn't that far from the boy where I was sitting. What I remember was that I was just seething; I was just really, really angry. In my head I was thinking how I could make a jump for him; I could go at him. I'm not that kind of person but I was seriously thinking about it but then I came to my senses. It didn't hit me right away but a couple of days after that. That convinced me that I hadn't really forgiven. It felt good in a fleshly way to be angry at him but it didn't feel right.*

All that time when she was in a coma and it seemed like there was no hope. The first glimmer of hope came when she was just getting out of that coma stage and having eye movements that were intentional. I was visiting her on a weekend and the nurses were working with her and they were saying, If you hear us, show us by holding up one or two fingers. That was the fist time I saw her purposely move her fingers. That was where I really got emotional and started crying.

Nothing sudden but it was just amazing all the little things that started coming back. The memories are much intact and now she can get around and live an independent life. The improvement in her speech was amazing in the first year. There was a time where every word was a struggle because her brain was not helping her. She probably sounds slow; she can talk so much more fluidly now than she could at first.

---

friends have suffered greatly; they are angry. They are frightened. But how will we survive over time? My children and I have shifted roles. My children have taken responsibility to make sure Mom is OK; they should be focusing on college, girl friends and having fun. This assault shook the foundations that I built with my kids. Support each other, be there for each other but live our own lives. Now they live my life. I have to learn how to reconnect with my family and friends. I have a new personality; I wish I did not have to be different. I know I can work but I will never function at my job. I used to type 100 words; now I type 3 words per minute. I used my verbal and organizational skills to sell, negotiate and manage. Now I cannot. I've been replaced at work. How am I going to function in this world? Why did this happen to me? I live in fear; I wonder if someone is going to get me. When I hear a strange noise I get scared. I have to tell myself no, no, don't let them rule my life. I pray every night that the doors are locked and that someone is not already inside. I keep a light on all the time. I constantly second-guess myself. I have a fear of living alone. The gunshot wound to my head made a difference in my life. You made a difference in my life. You have damaged me and my family physically, emotionally and mentally. You not only stole my car and purse, but you stole my life. You took away my security and belief in mankind. As a mother I want to say why, why, how could you do this? There is so much hurt. I don't remember the day I was shot. I don't remember what my life was all about. All I know is that when you shot me you changed the course of my life forever.

She is a different person. Sometimes I miss that old self and sometimes I miss what she was like. She wasn't very emotional before the accident. When she was married she was not emotional, either publicly or within the family. She got to the point late in the marriage feeling like she couldn't share her emotions. If I saw her cry I would get scared. After the divorce she would occasionally express sadness. On a scale of 10, she was a 2 or 3 in showing emotion. Now she is body-expressive in her passion. When she gets wired she stands up and paces back and forth. She loves doing her speaking engagements; they drive her and give her focus.

But she was always very loving even though she wasn't emotional. There are some people who are unemotional and do not say they love you. She could always express love but it was the other side of the emotions that she didn't show – the crying and anger. I think she labeled them negative. There are some things that don't change.

I was 15 when she got divorced. My Mom and I were pretty close. We did a lot of things together. Walking together. She would come and watch me umpire softball. A funny thing I remember about that whole time, I was barely 16 and she had just had a hysterectomy. It was elaborate and she was down and pretty much on the couch and unable to do much. I was going to get some ice cream and bring it back and so I took her car – I'd only had my license for about three months – I totaled her Ford Taurus (maroon). I wasn't paying attention and smashed it. The horn went off and stayed on. I wasn't as nervous about the car as I was about telling her about it, especially in her condition. The policeman followed me home because I didn't have my license with me. The car was leaking oil all over the place but somehow it still ran. I was starting to cry on the way home because I was freaked out about telling my mom. I was sobbing, I totaled your car, *and she was saying it was alright, it was alright. I wasn't so concerned about her being mad but that she would be so worried about me and that she would hurt herself in her condition. She called her sister and brother-in-law and they helped deal with me. That was a weird moment; we were close that way and she was obviously very concerned about me.*

She was in the hospital full time until March or April. She was released to be home. When she got home I felt like more of her caretaker. I was still in school. There were a lot of support people. I was obviously in and out during school. I was home that spring. Then is when it really felt like a burden at times. It felt like it was all on me. That frustrated me.

I must have been getting to the end of my rope that spring. (I took an engineering co-op job in May – in Clintonville – that lasted all the way until January.) A couple of my friends came over on a weekend and they knew I just needed to get away. They took me to Pizza Hut and I vented to them. They listened. It took my mind off it a bit; that one night it felt good. I love my Mom but it was frustrating taking care of her too. Maybe that spring I was feeling like, oh man, what am I going to do over the summer? If I stay home my life is going to be all about that; I needed an engineering co-op to advance myself too.

Mom went through a bunch of physical therapy outside the hospital. She actually lived in a place that gave her a lot of therapy; she didn't really like the structured life and at the time she didn't like having roommates. She likes solitude and she wasn't getting it. She was getting antsy to get out. When she came home to her condo she was still in rough shape. She could see well enough to get around, she could walk, and she got her meals somehow. I kept thinking that her life could have been so different.

Derek and I talk about the links among Craig, Josh and Jackie. The word *intimacy* comes up – the idea that the three of them have a connection from sharing the experience of the shooting that no one else ever can truly understand.

Intimacy…that is something I have always wondered too. They have something that nobody else can really understand or have knowledge of. I just…it doesn't bother me quite as much any more. I didn't want to think about that whole situation. I can't imagine what she thought about. She would be the first person to give up everything if she was held up. We always talked about what ifs before. If she was getting robbed – she couldn't have cared less about the material things – she wasn't going to be a hero. I know she was not an aggressor in this thing at all. I can't imagine what these kids were thinking either. I just don't get it. They just set themselves up for the whole thing. They just went right into the house; with guns; and maybe it wasn't part of their preconceived plan to shoot someone, but I almost think it was because they were carrying guns. It wasn't that they needed the guns to get a car. It was only her peering out at them that made them the aggressors. It was accounts from their teachers that made me think they were looking for something – a thrill or rebellion but they were definitely looking for some trouble and they got it. I can understand rage, I've been there too. But that wasn't what it was for them. I don't understand.

Derek's two daughters are being put to bed and each one comes quietly into the living room to hug their Dad goodnight. They look shyly at me. Derek

Derek, Jackie and Jackie's granddaughter, after
the shooting

reassures them that they can be together as a family all day the next day – Saturday. There are small leaps of joy, contained because of the stranger in the room. Before I leave, we talk about the daughters, Jackie's grandchildren.

Even my five-year-old really doesn't have a sense of what happened. That is just Grandma. That is always who she was; she has some special bond with her Grandma and she may just sense that Grandma is a little more fragile. Always the first thing she wants to do is climb up on her lap and just cuddle. Our younger daughter is three and rarely wants to cuddle; she just wants to run around. She has never brought up any questions.

Eventually they are going to know the whole reality and that will be a tough one to talk through with them, I think.

The interview ends. I walk down the dark stairs toward my car. In the nearby downtown area I can hear families at the outdoor ice cream shop talking about the big game. There is no click of a door lock behind me.

SON · CHAD

Chad joins us in Jackie's apartment just days before he and his girlfriend, Lisa, move to Pennsylvania. In answer to the question, *Who was your Mom before she was hurt?* Chad's first words are about her independence and strong will. *She was a great Mom, generous and supportive of everything I ever did.* She *allowed me to make my own mistakes. She was easygoing.*

She did not want to be a best friend to her sons, but we could tell her things and not be afraid of her reaction. She was always there for us. When the track team used 100 rolls of toilet paper to decorate a local home, Chad took Jackie to see their masterpiece. Her reaction? Impressed!

During Chad's senior year in high school Jackie lent him her new red Honda Civic to take his buddies to see the Pro-Football Hall of Fame in Canton, Ohio, a trip of more than 1000 miles. After all, Walter Payton was a recent inductee.

Not many parents would send their son, who had been driving for only a couple of years, off in their new car but Mom did. She trusted me and knew I'd do well. I did.

The core of her personality has stayed the same. Deep down, she remains forgiving and generous and is even stronger than she was before. There are aspects of a person even a bullet cannot erase.

Chad is slight and soft spoken. An introvert. A cross-country runner. A high school math teacher. His short hair cut reveals the scars from a brain surgery he had about ten years ago. *I was so sick as a kid. I had an autoimmune disease and was hospitalized hundreds of times. I had 13 or 14 surgeries before I was 16. Mom was there after every surgery and always spent the nights with me, sleeping in a chair – except for one time and ironically that is my most vivid memory of being afraid in the hospital. Going to the hospital wasn't unusual and hospitals were not a bad place to me.*

Just before one of the high school cross country meets, I crashed my buddy's moped. I landed head first on concrete. My teammates honored me by writing my initials in tape on their track shoes. And after my brain surgery half of the team came into my intensive care room. They sat everywhere, one even sat on the commode, not knowing what it was. Mom said she knew I was going to be OK when she saw how I lit up at seeing my friends. I got the thirty staples taken out of my head on my birthday and came home to a surprise party my Mom threw for me. It was just what I needed. Mom always paid attention to the little things.

And then there was the camcorder. Mom loved that camera and filmed us all the time, even when I was dressing for my prom. She missed nothing, misses nothing! Chad and Jackie laugh.

For one of the cross-country meets, she walked out on the field to film the start of the race. The camera was running when the referee fired the starter's pistol. Mom was so startled by the sound she dropped the camera while it was still running. We have a film of grass. Happily it was a false start and she was ready for the second shot that actually began the race.

When we move on to Chad's memories of the events that followed his mom's injury, the words are staccato, rapid fire. His memory is vivid as are personal memories of all moments of profound change where emotion and intellect meld. The story sounds memorized. I know it is a permanent imprint; a brand that will forever remain part of this young man's being in the same ways the bullet fragments remain part of his mother's brain.

It was a weekend – a Sunday morning – my freshman year of college. Some high school friends were visiting. We were planning to go out to breakfast with my Dad and brother. Something had seemed off to me the day before – Saturday; I was down all day. At 8am my brother called me. We were at the same college. He said, Dad called. We have to go home. Mom is in the hospital.

We did not know why. We drove together and barely talked, each with our own thoughts and concerns. A million things were going through my head.

We went to the Verona condo where we spent time with Mom on weekends. Dad and Grandma were standing outside. They had no key. We knew it was serious because they were both there. We opened the door and sat down inside. Grandma and Dad sat on the couch and we sat in the chairs.

Grandma told us Mom had been visiting John at the tree farm. In my mind I kept trying to finish her story quickly. I was imagining an animal attack – a bear, maybe. I was wrong.

There weren't many details: a nap, the garage, the car, a gunshot.

I felt nothing. I was numb. I had no reaction to the news. My brain said, Huh?

I was not sad.

I was not angry.

Grandma said we needed to go to the hospital but first, did Mom have a will? We dug around in her papers, looking. It felt so strange to be going through Mom's papers.

All the relatives were at the hospital when we arrived. The doctor took us aside, with my Dad and Grandma. He showed us brain x-rays. Bullet fragments were all over the picture. He said there was no real chance of life continuing and that we should get Mom's affairs in order.

The next days are a blur. The first time I cried was when I returned home and began to tell my friends what had happened. Mom was on life support. She was unconscious.

Some nights I would go to the hospital in the early morning hours. No one else was around. No family, no media. I just wanted to be alone with Mom. I wanted to tell her things – all the things I had done. Confessions, I guess. I did not know what I was feeling and I needed to figure it out with her even though I knew she couldn't hear me.

Life went on.

My family encouraged me to return to school and I did but I did not attend classes other than physical education and ceramics. School seemed trivial and unimportant. My roommate, a long time friend, understood. He knew me. He listened.

My friends were so important. A group of us had been friends since we were little kids. We had played football together but, Chad laughs, *they used me AS the football when we played. I was so small then.*

DEPRESSION AND THOUGHTS OF SUICIDE

In May or June of 1996 – seven months after the accident – I thought about suicide, Jackie explains with no visible emotion. *I thought that my kids had to be so tired of having to be my parent. They had to be so tired. And I was tired of all of the rehab work.*

During my recovery, I realized that my sons were my parents. Jackie pauses and puts her left fist to her chest. *I don't like my sons being my parents; I want to scream it to the world. I can feel they are my parents and I want to shout,* You aren't my parents. *But I couldn't do a thing to tell them. It was locked away inside of me. You know I wanted them to think about college. I wanted them to have friends. Everything inside of me – that is what I wanted. But outside, I was a child. I couldn't do my books. I couldn't cook. I couldn't clean. I couldn't do all the things that I did before the accident. They had to worry about me; it was the parent/child thing.*

My older son had to do the finances. He had to make the decisions. Derek said he went out one night with some friends and he told them he wanted to be the son. He wasn't mad at me. He wasn't mad at **me**. He was mad at what Craig and Josh did. *They took away his mother and gave him a child.* Derek talked to an interviewer who asked if I was going to live. *He could have said,* We love her so much that she got better. *He didn't. He said,* She did it for us – her sons. We are all so close.

The parent/child piece was the most important thing I had in my life. It was to be the mother. It was to be the mother to Chad and Derek. I am so proud of them. I can't say it enough. I love them; they will always live in my heart and I will always live in their hearts. Some people have said that I spoiled my kids. So?

I taught them about love. I taught them about boundaries. The time my son stole from a store and I made him go with me and apologize and he did. He did a grand job, so much so that the general manager offered him a job.

Jackie sits silently for a moment before continuing. *But I thought about doing away with myself. I was so tired of doing all the work. I was tired. I was sorry that my sons had to be the adults and I had it all planned out. I knew I wouldn't kill myself by a bullet.* Jackie laughs. *I knew; no bullet. I would buy pills. I had it all planned out within 24 hours. But then I made a call to Derek. He answered the phone and we talked and he said that even if I were a vegetable, at least he would have a mother. Those words resonated. I couldn't commit suicide. I knew it then, I know it now. He has a mother.* Jackie's words are measured. *His mother has changed but he wants me around.*

It is hard to be alive; it is hard getting up each morning and doing the things I have to do. It is hard but it is what I have been dealt. You know, people nowadays, they jump out of bed. They do this. They do that. I can't do it that way. This hand, Jackie is holding her right hand out, *it is really asleep. I can hold things in this pocket,* she indicates her thumb and forefinger. *But that is about it. You know this stove…it is my archenemy.* Jackie puts her left hand on the cold electric burner next to her; she cannot cook because she doesn't remember that the burner is turned on. Her two aides work a total of 20 hours a week doing her chores and taking her places.

I have had to do things in alternative ways. I have come a long way but I will remember – not remember because I don't remember – November 4 at 4:40 for the rest of my life. I know why it happened. I believe that God thought I could handle a new life. I have opened up my heart to Craig and Josh. I have talked, talked, talked. I think God is proud of me for doing it.

PITY PARTY FOR ONE

I occasionally have to have a pity party for one. I feel sorry for myself. I get mad. I am not proud of my pity parties. I know, I know, I know – I have every right to feel pity but I prided myself into thinking that the world was A-OK and the people in it were OK. I think that, early on in my recovery, I was sad for the first time in my life. I was angry, so angry that Craig and Josh tried to kill me. I was so angry that I had a pity party but I only invited me. I was the only one allowed to see it and to attend.

At the party, I have anything I want to eat. It is freeing. I am whoever I want to be during that time and I do it alone. I want to be alone with my thoughts. I want to be alone with my anger; my sadness. It isn't a matter of others not understanding but they… I feel they would interfere with how I feel and how I am.

I go to my most favorite restaurant and I can have whatever I want. I could have Honey Dijon sauce with my sandwich. [I can't spell Dijon…Jackie says, *d-i-j-o-n.*] *I could have the seasoned French fries and a Coke. And then I would have a dessert – a cheesecake, something dribbled on top like strawberries. I would eat it leisurely. I would then get up from the table and walk home. I walked to and from. It was about two miles. And the food and the company would dissipate…ah, ha, I do know big words. It would make my feelings of sadness and anger go away. I just needed a little time to get through it. If I had tears, I had tears. I just got through.*

Jackie pauses and I add, *This seems very positive.*

It is even when I talk about it now, it is good for me to express my feelings. It is good for me to express them and be over them.

I nod. *It is a thing you can control.*

When I tell you about the accident, it is raw. But you, just now, you have allowed me to have my pity party and you're still sitting there. Kudos to you!!

So many things are gone away from me but I am richer. I have met so many people; I have met so many. My sons both say they like me more but I know what answer they are going to give. The old Jackie is dead and the new one is here. They didn't have any choice.

⊰——⋈——⊱

Outside my third floor Isla Mujeres' hotel window, frigate birds are still,
suspended – as poet Mary Oliver[7] says – *high in the clean blue air.*
Like angular weathervanes, they face the breezes coming off of the ocean,
a block distant from where I sit. They are fixed in time. They epitomize
freedom. My hotel room is larger than a prison cell. But not by much.
And yet I get to type and edit and walk past fishermen stringing out nets
at dawn and sit sipping strong coffee in this lovely January heat.
I awaken in the coolness of the silent night with thoughts about Jackie's
story and I get up and turn on lights and type. I laugh. I cry. Having such
unrestricted freedom and privilege seems paradoxical in choreographing
this story affecting so many people's lives, three of whom – Jackie, Craig
and Josh – are imprisoned by the unreflective acts of a moment in time.

⊰——⋈——⊱

THE BOYS THAT DID IT TO ME, AND THEY WERE JUST BOYS...

Not all aspects of Jackie's presentations to youth, adults, prisoners, police and
students stay the same. But there are two lines that never vary. They are: ...*the
boys that did it to me, and they were just boys. They were 15 and 16 years old.*

Jackie requests letters from Craig and Josh answering a series of questions we
develop. Both respond quickly. Following are their letters, in full, with annota-
tions from Jackie in ***bold italics*** – her responses as I read the letters aloud to her.

CRAIG'S LETTER ON THE SHOOTING

⊰——⋈——⊱

He was always a good boy; a polite boy.

– Comment from Craig's grandmother at his sentencing hearing.

⊰——⋈——⊱

Question #1:
In as much detail as you possibly can, tell us what you remember about the
day Jackie was shot. What did you do? What did she do?

---

[7] Oliver, Mary (1992). "Wild Geese." *New and Selected Poems.* Boston: Beacon Press. P. 110.

Craig, in his teen years.

First off I should say that I have been trying to forget that day ever since it happened so some details have blurred, thankfully.

Jackie comments: He is glad it is blurry, all the facts, but I'm not. I wish they would remember. I don't have recall; I don't have the knowledge that they had. It is all blank to me and I feel, um, not stupid but I feel, Jackie struggles for the word, I feel that I can't even remember the simple things. For instance, did I cry – I know I didn't. What did I say? I can't remember. It is that I can't remember that is driving me to drink – if I could. People say it is good I can't remember. It is good, maybe, but it sure does a number on me. I have read their statements; I have asked Craig and Josh questions. But I don't remember a thing.

Why is it important that you remember, I ask. **I will say I – peaceful. It would be peaceful because I want to remember everything but I don't want to remember the fear.**

We return to reading Craig's letter: *The day started off with Josh and I at his house. We had some vague idea of running away from home but no plan as people have said. We had the clothes on our backs and next to no money. All we had was a desire to leave. Actually, I should say that I had a desire to just disappear (sp?), leave. I can't speak for Josh as I don't know what he was thinking so when I say "we" I only mean that he was there as well.*

I feel so sad for Josh and Craig. I feel sad.

Someone took us to Reedsburg, I believe it was one of Josh's parents. Once we got to town we started walking around, aimlessly. Eventually it was decided to find Mike … and see if he wanted to go with us. We walked around for a while, couldn't find him. At some point it was decided to steal some guns from my mother's boyfriend's gun cabinet. We went over to Mike's house again and nobody was home so we took a duffle bag from Mike's room to put the guns in.

We went back to my Mom's place and I proceeded to break the back of the gun cabinet and stole the two pistols. After a little while we left. On the way out my Mom's boyfriend came in and gave me a bit of a start as I had no conscious clue as to what in the name of anything I was doing. We cut across this empty cornfield and headed into town. Once in town, we proceeded aimlessly around for a while then decided to hide the guns and see if we could find Mike. We walked around for what seemed like forever, it was pretty cold. Mike was eventually found. We asked him if he wanted to go with us, we tried to convince him but, thank God, he continued to say no.

I think about that and I have nothing but respect for Mike because, in my opinion, one of the hardest things for a kid to do is say "no" to friends in almost any situation, even if you know the situation is wrong. He showed a lot of courage and honor. I am proud of him for that.

Craig shows, oh Jesus, what to say, Craig sees that Mike was right and he gives him credit for not coming. It breaks my heart that he couldn't see that too. He was in pain.

Jackie and I return to our slow reading of Craig's letter: *After we left Mike, we went back and got the guns. Then we started walking towards the country, why I have no idea. Some cars passed and Josh suggested we flag down one and just shoot the people. I said no and I guess that was enough to end the idea. We kept walking for a long time, eventually walking past the house where Jackie was at. We walked a ways past the residence and decided to go back to the residence since there was a car in the open garage.*

I remember an excerpt from Craig's recorded testimony in court that relates to this moment in the story:

Q Where did you go from there, from in the garage?
A To the door.
Q Did you look at the car, at that time?
A Not that I remember. I don't think that I did. I don't know if I did or not, but I don't think that I did.
Q Why were you going to that house?
A I have no clue. You know, for the car, but I never looked into the car. I don't know why.
Q Did you think that the car keys weren't in the car?
A I don't know. Like I said, I didn't even, you know, think about looking into the car. I really didn't know what was going on, at this point.

– Craig's testimony, Criminal Complaint, State of Wisconsin Circuit Court, Sauk County, pp. 405-406

And Jackie comments on this section of Craig's letter as well: *He saw my car. My beautiful Honda that wasn't paid for. They had decided to steal it. Jackie laughs. The beautiful red Honda LX: candy apple red. My younger son, when he got his car, he got a Honda Civic LX and he said to me he wanted to get it candy apple red and I said, No. There is only one. And so he got a black one. Mine was candy apple red; there should be no others.*

I continue reading Craig's letter aloud to Jackie: *We walked in and took out the guns. I don't remember how that decision was made but we pulled them out. I had the .44 and Josh had the .22. I rang the doorbell a few times and nobody came out so we went in the house. I don't remember if I went in first or if Josh did. Once in the house I walked around and checked the rooms. The first room was empty so I went to the next room. Jackie was in there sleeping so I closed the door and told Josh that we need to go. So we went out to the garage. I walked around to the driver's side of the car and as I was about to get in, Jackie came out. Jackie asked us if we needed something and I said, "No, we already have what we need." Then Josh and I pointed the guns at Jackie and told her to get into the house.*

Craig has said he wouldn't do it over again, Jackie interjects. *He wouldn't do my injuries over again. He doesn't know it but he is learning to love. It is something he needed all along. I would like to say it WITH MEANING because this is what I think. He was becoming a young man, from a boy to a young man, when I met him the first time. It was December 17, 1997. He was a boy but I have watched him become a young man. My sons became young men, became loving young men. I wouldn't have to teach them the loving part. I have with Craig. He used to be a boy that was searching for love.*

And from the letter, *She went into the house and we followed. Jackie was told to lay on the ground and she did. I believe she said "Please don't hurt me." I told her that I wouldn't and went to this little island area and asked Josh what we were going to do. Neither of us knew, I guess. I set the .44 down directly in front of me, directly. Josh set his gun down in a similar fashion. I said "directly" because it's at this point where I started to feel as though I was watching myself, like I wasn't really doing what I was doing.*

*Josh said, "Who's going to do it" and I think I said I would. I then reached **across** Josh, not to the gun **directly** in front of me and grabbed the .22. Why I do not know. I walked into the living room, a pillow was retrieved from someplace, I put the pillow over Jackie's head and shot her. Then we left. Josh got into the car. I got in. Then we drove off. At some point we pulled off to the side of the road and threw out Jackie's purse. Then we started to drive aimlessly. I was sick and in shock. We decided to go and find something to eat. I still have no idea why but I felt like I was starving at that point.*

Jackie is living these moments with Craig. ***He was feeling remorse. He was being eaten alive with regret.***

We got to Mauston, I believe it was Mauston at least, stopped at McDonalds, got some food. I opened my food up and almost threw up. I was nowhere near hungry. We drove around, aimlessly, somehow it was decided to ditch the car and go to my Mom's house. It was also decided to burn the car, no idea where that came from. We eventually got a gas can and gas. We drove out a ways from my Mom's place, parked the car and set it on fire. As we were leaving someone in a truck came by and asked us what in the hell were we doing. I don't remember what my reply was. The guy pulled off and we ran, eventually made it to my Mom's and I lay down, sick, tired, exhausted. The cops eventually came and that was it.

I pause in the reading and Jackie adds, ***I think I feel as tired and as worn out as Craig did. I think, um, he couldn't eat or drink because he kept remembering he shot me. I am his worst nightmare. You think about everything and you can't figure out why he had shot me. I think he was a young man who felt everyone hated him so he hated everyone. I think from that moment on we would be together, no not together, we would be connected. No matter how hard we try to not be, we will be connected. And I say "we;" he was going to throw up when he thought of me. He went home and he was in bed thinking about me. It is sad. Sad.***

*In answering this question I don't mean to sound cold or like I don't care what I did. I am sorry I did this and I hate writing it down. I hate thinking about it. Thankfully the details are hazy. You wanted it in detail for your book so don't judge me as a 'monster' because of the way it sounds. Jackie didn't want to put her kids through this again and I **completely** understand that as I continually try to forget that day yet I write this and have to relive it.*

I, for over ten years, have not written a book; basically for Chad and Derek. And I didn't even think about Craig and Josh. I hope that Craig can forgive himself for telling the story. I am writing this story in the hope that people will think about their choices. I hope that he will see the good that it will do. When you write a book, you think that it will only affect your kids then you stop and think about all the others.

Question # 2:
As you know, Jackie talks to many groups about the shooting and her subsequent, immediate forgiveness. She says, I love the boys. I love Craig and Josh. How do you react to this? How do you react to Jackie's love?

It is a very strange thing having the person you hurt, almost caused to die, to say they forgive you first of all but to have them say they love you still blows my mind when I think about it because that is 180 degrees from normal in today's world. At times it is uncomfortable but most of the time it feels good to know Jackie has forgiven me and her love for me has helped me to forgive myself a little for what I did. I react to her love the only way I can, with gratitude.

Jackie responds, *Hmm, with gratitude. What does gratitude mean? Thankfulness. Hmm. I don't care if they never forgive themselves but if they can grow beyond that I think that is important. If they can forgive themselves, I think that is powerful for them. I want them to never hurt someone as they did me. And if it takes them not forgiving themselves, so be it. But they can rise above it. At the last yearly visit with Craig, I asked what he'd like to do when he is released. He said he has changed so much. He said before that he would go to every Green Bay Packers game, but he now thinks that he would like to go to the homeland of his father. He would like to get a job with – something that begins with the letter p – p – where they go in and build homes – Habitat for Humanity. And he would like to do the work that I am doing. That is the kind of thing I look for in him.*

I ask Jackie to clarify. *Even though you have forgiven him, you don't want to instill forgiveness in him?*

It sounds so much more horrible when you say it. I don't mean...I think that they should look above it and, um, should look above it. If they would look above it...it's like, if they say they forgive themselves, did they learn anything? I don't know. Saying they forgive themselves could just be an easy out for them.

But it is better if they remember what they did, OK, remember it, but they can do so much better. They say what can we do, we are in prison? But you can do wonderful things in prison. You know, they have written letters that I have read to the audiences where they are thinking of all the boys and girls, of the adults. They offer their point of view. They have jobs. They may not think that they are very good jobs, but they have jobs and earn money, granted it is little but it is still something. They earn money for themselves to buy toothpaste, deodorant, anything they might need. They could be using their parents' money but they aren't. They are using their money.

Question #3:
Did you believe Jackie had forgiven you? Do you believe it now? Why?

Once I met Jackie for the first time in Green Bay [prison] I believed she forgave me by her not trying to berate (sp?) me in any form. Then she said she forgave me. Yes, I still believe it now. Jackie has said she forgives me and her letters and occasional visits help confirm her words.

He thought I would not try and see him or write him. I thought that if one of my sons had done it, what would they expect? They would expect me to love them. They would expect me to care about them. If one of my sons had tried to kill a woman, I wouldn't like the fact of what they did but I would still love them.

It is kind of like when you have a child. That child is with you no matter what. They are with me till death do us part. I could or they could not see me but I'd be with them in their mind every waking moment. I am with the boys in their prison cells. I am with them when they work. I am with them every moment. I forgive them; I'm neither right nor wrong. I could have hated them. I could have been scared of them. I could have been plotting revenge on them. Neither right nor wrong. My actions are no better than someone else's actions because they are what I felt; what I FEEL. I can't say it clearly for you because it is feelings I feel for them.

I am reminded of Derek's and my conversation about the intimacy Craig, Josh and Jackie share from the moment of the shooting: just the three of them there. Only Craig and Josh remember exactly what happened. No one else can know the full range of emotion and intensity of that moment. I speak the thought aloud to Jackie. *There is an intimacy you, Craig and Josh share. No one else can go where the three of you have been together. No one else will ever truly understand the moments you lived together. And you cannot remember them.*

Others can try to go to where Josh, Craig and I have been. Others cannot answer because they haven't been there. It is MY feelings. It is Josh's. It is Craig's. Only the three of us can truthfully say.

Question #4:
How have you changed as a result of all that has happened to you since the shooting?

Craig writes, *I believe over time I am becoming a man through constant striving towards growth and development. I am more understanding of things in life. I am maturing. I appreciate everything more now than before. I have a drive to be someone, to make a difference in life, to be someone people can look to as a good person.*

I've also become more bitter towards certain people or I should say administration and certain people can treat fellow human beings like trash. We have messed up to get here, yes, but we're still human. I get more compassion from the lady I shot than some people that run these prisons and from the people that send people to these prisons. I was a 16-year-old kid that messed up badly, yet, I'm thrown to the wolves. I can understand the need for punishment but I can't rationalize certain things, I don't know, I guess.

Overall, I believe I am a better, more well-rounded, strong-willed young man from all of my experiences over these last almost eleven years. It is my hope to continue to grow and one day be a man.

Jackie shakes her head. *But what a price. You know, you sit and think: he was a 16-year-old boy that had been on this earth for 16 years and did not know the meaning of love. He didn't know about boundaries.*

CRAIG'S RESPONSES TO JACKIE'S QUESTIONS

In addition to the questions Jackie and I developed for Craig and Josh, Jackie asked them both to respond to a series of more personal questions.

Why do you hug me when you first see me at our visitations?

I guess that is the best way to say that you care about someone. At the same time it is a way to say I'm sorry, even if it is a small gesture. I also have to believe that you don't hate me because would you give me a hug in return if you did hate me?

Why did you show me tears when I told you I was worried about my son who was vacationing in London after the bombing?

I understand and accept that your sons more likely than not hate me or if the hate has subsided they just have an extreme dislike for me – both cases being normal and expected I would guess. I've internalized this fact and expected it as a part of life. Having said that I feel no ill will towards them – I have no reason to – things have taken their course and our lives are linked together. We all have played our part. I know now how important those boys are to you. They're also important to me in some way that I can't explain fully. So it hit me to see you going through even more than you've already endured. Thankfully everything turned out well. Pretty long winded answer, eh?

Why did you sign the statement that you would pay me a million dollars?

*I am sorry for what I have done to you. I'm trying in whatever way I can to say I'm sorry, to prove it. I want you, your family, my family, **everyone** to know I'm sorry and I'm not some beast like I was labeled. If I have to give you whatever money I have to prove this I guess I'll be trying to prove it for the rest of my life.*

><><

At the sentencing hearing, Josh's mother said,
He just fell through the cracks.

><><

JOSH'S RESPONSES TO JACKIE'S QUESTIONS

Josh also responded to Jackie's more personal questions to him. Below are his answers. Again, Jackie's reactions to the letters I read aloud to her are in ***bold italics*** in the text.

Dear Jackie:

Hi, I'm doing pretty good. How are you doing?

Josh, in his teen years.

I'm going to do my best to answer your questions for your book, which I'm happy to be a part of. As for your letters, I'll try to get those written as well. It's a lot of emotional stuff to write, and it's not really a lot of time, but I'll do my best to get them out on time.

So, here's an answer to your questions for the book.

You asked why I am nervous when we meet. My answer's based on our first meeting.

Of course the biggest reason I was nervous is that I'm coming face to face with the person whose life I had a part in destroying! I had no idea how you'd react to seeing me, considering all the things I believe you were told concerning why I hadn't met with you till then. I read the newspaper articles, most were very untrue. I never denied my guilt or refused to meet with you. I couldn't because I was going back to court on appeal. Then I was shipped out of state for five years. At which point we started corresponding through letters to each other. So I thought you might be angry or hostile towards me. Keeping in mind that most of the emotional issues I deal with [with] others in here revolve around anger and hostility. So I tend to think people will react in this manner.

It is when he looked into my eyes the first time we met, I knew he was sorry. I think both of them are guilty of my attempted murder. He did not shoot me but he stole the gun, he had held a gun over me, he drove my car, he helped set my car on fire. At one point he could have done something – call 911? – but he didn't. I feel sad about Josh. He has got the prisons now being his parents and for that I'm sorry.

Your next question is "what's different about me since you were shot."

That's a big question. Most of who I am now is nothing like I was then. Some of my personality traits are still the same, sense of humor, ability to get along with others. I was a disgruntled teenager who couldn't see past my own confused emotions. I've had to grow up in an environment of crime, violence and lost control. But I choose early on that I'd distance myself from all those things to the best of my abilitys. No one can get away from those things completely, I certainly haven't been able to. Some things, violence mostly, is forced on you in here. But I've done my best to

shape myself into a good person, an intelligent person. I've gotten as much educa-
tion as I've been able. I've become a Christian, going so far as to take college cours-
es from a Bible school. And in general I've tried to do the right thing in all my deci-
sions and choices in my life. So I guess you could say I've grown up a lot, and I'm
a completely new person from the lost boy who was a part of a horrible decision and
terrible crime. Someday I'll be given a second chance at life and I can assure you
I'll make the most of it!

It is sad to think that it took almost killing me to get him to stop and think
about all of these things in his life. It is sad to think he thought that by beat-
ing up somebody, it would make him feel better. I would ask him factiously,
how did that work for him? That is funny. That is funny Jackie bends at waist
and slaps her leg. *It is funny because I just think that I can picture him ask-*
ing me about love and forgiveness and I would say, you know, how do you give
love and forgiveness? I don't know the answer. You just do. I have forgiveness
for many, many, many people. When I go in to a prison the inmates look at
me and see their victims. I have yet to figure that out. They will openly cry in
front of me. Openly cry. I think it is them crying in front of their victim. I used
to think it was helpful to have my right side paralyzed and be legitimately...
I mean legally blind. It isn't that. It is because they see so much in my eyes.

One person had a question and he couldn't get it out because he was crying so
hard. My last prison presentation, the inmates gave me a standing ovation
and they kept clapping and clapping. I had my hat on and I wanted to pull
it down over my face. They weren't clapping for me; I was just the messenger.
I am but a messenger. A woman inmate from Minnesota wrote me and she
wanted my forgiveness. Jackie puts her hand over her mouth and stands in
silence. *MY forgiveness.*

Your last question is: what have I learned?

Mostly I've learned how to gain control over my emotions, which helps in making
good, intelligent choices, instead of impulsive or emotional responses to things. This
I believe has been instrumental in changing from who I was to who I've become.
In here it's much easier to be like most in here, and react emotionally to things. But
that generally leads to problems, not solutions. I guess you could say I've learned
who I really am! That life is hard, and unfair mostly, but that we must make the
best of each situation and live to the best of our abilities! And things usually turn
out pretty good in the end.

You know, life it is good, it is bad. You have to take it. Some is bad, some is bad. I have…but you know I think I live in a glass house – I don't know if I want to live in a glass house – I look at life a different way. It's – rose-colored glasses…that is what I meant to say. I wear rose-colored glasses. I choose my rose-colored glasses. But I wanted to meet the two boys, granted under nicer terms, but meet them nevertheless, I have. I am proud of them. I am proud of them for what they are doing. Craig is 27 and Josh is 26 and they have turned into fine young men. I would be proud of having them at each and every talk I give.

That's the answers to your personal questions. Jackie, I hope it's what you are looking for. If you need them to be longer or more detailed let me know and I'll try.

Sincerely, Josh

JOSH'S LETTER ON THE SHOOTING

—————✕—————

At the sentencing hearing, Josh said,
I'll never forgive myself for being there that day.

—————✕—————

Josh writes his version of the series of events surrounding the shooting: *I guess I'll start at the beginning, which is what drove me to get involved in this whole thing.*

I was 15 years old. And I liked to think of myself as tough. To that end I was always eager to get into fights, or cause general trouble. Of course I'd try to keep this from resulting in me getting caught. So I was pretty well behaved at home and at school.

When I met Craig it was about 7-8 months before the Incident. He had a car, and I was having problems with my parents on the Issue of getting my license. So that was the main reason we became friends. At first it was just general stuff, going out to have fun, that sort of thing. But like most kids our age, we had a lot of emotional turmoil. Things that seemed so huge, world ending things. Such as my license. This made me angry, and that I was fairly poor, we didn't starve, but it was bad seeming at the time. I had a lot of anger, and I started directing it at everyone, even if they weren't the real problem.

Eventually I found that Craig had similar thoughts and problems as I did. This got us to talking about crime and how we didn't care what happened because no one loved us. Originally the plan we occasional talked on was just random ideas. And then shortly before the Incident, we came up with the plan to steal a car and rob a bank. Nothing grand. Just a small Farm's bank, with a couple of employees. We didn't really plan it out, beyond the need for a stolen car, and guns.

November 1, 1995. Recent events had conspired to push us over the edge. I was having problems with my girlfriend, which at that time was the only reason we'd been putting off doing anything. Craig was ready to go whenever, I think because his life was worse than mine, or so it seemed at the time. Anyway, we talked, I was hurting so I said screw it let's go ahead and do it. He came over to my house about 2 days later, the 3rd. I'd been on a no sleep thing since the 1st, so I was on day three of no sleep when he showed up. I'm not very hard to convince to do dumb things when I've a lack of sleep. My self control is gone. Basically I had reservations, but in that state I didn't care about consequences. So when he just showed up that night and asked if I was still down, I told him sure. So we hung out for a few more hours till morning, then I convinced my Dad to take us to Craig's house, which was in a different town. After we got there, Craig brought up the need for guns if we were going to rob the bank, so we went to his place where his mom's boyfriend kept some guns. We broke into the gun cabinet and stole one gun, .44 caliber revolver. And Craig took the .22 caliber from a desk, like a file cabinet type. I also took a hunting knife, because I had a knife collection, and it was a cool looking hunting knife. After that we decided to go look for a car, one that had keys in it. We went all over the place, to the shopping stores and factories but we couldn't find anything with keys. After about 4 hours Craig took me to Subway where his friend Mike worked. We ate and then Craig told Mike we needed some money, so we waited for him to get off work. Before then we took the guns which were in a duffel bag, and hid them in the woods behind the local school. When he got off work, Craig took us back to the woods to show him the guns, ask for money, and try to get him to come with us. After about a half-hour of trying, he refused. Craig pulled me to the side and asked if I thought he should shoot Mike, so that he wouldn't tell on us. We talked and then made Mike agree or promise not to say anything or even that he'd seen us at all that day. He agreed and then gave us like $40.00. Then he went home and we went looking for a car again. By this time it was get pretty late, and I'd hurt my leg, so I was limping and wanted to give up. Craig said he new one more place to look, a bar right outside of town. I agreed after a time and we went off down some country road. When we got to the bar it was closed or at least there wasn't any cars. Again I wanted to give up, but Craig wanted to keep going, looking for a house where no one was home. By this point I was tired and just didn't care so I agreed to look for 1 more hour.

It was shortly there after when we spotted a house with no lights on. And there was a car in the garage. We decided to do the ol' knock on the door and ask for a fake person if anyone answered the door. We rang the door bell several times and knocked twice, and when no one answered the door, we figured no one was home. I tried the door, and found it was unlocked. We went in, to what turned out as a kitchen. The goal was to find the keys for the car. Craig wandered off while I looked around the kitchen. I found a purse on the floor, that was unzipped and a set of keys were right on top. I picked up the purse and sat it on a counter. At that point Craig came from down the hall and whispered that someone was in a back bedroom sleeping. I showed him the keys and said let's go before we get caught. So we left and Craig took the keys and was unlocking the car when a voice behind us asked, "Can I help you?" We both looked around, and saw a woman standing in the doorway. Craig answered, "No, we have what we want." Craig pulled his gun, and then I followed suit. I told her "come out here." Craig yelled, "No, go inside." Then came around the car and followed her into the house. The woman said "Please don't hurt me." She repeated this several times, then Craig told her to lie on the floor, and put her hands behind her back. He then left. She repeated her earlier statement. I told her, "Don't worry, we're not going to hurt you, we just want the car." She then said, "Please don't steal my car, it's new and I'm still paying for it." Right then Craig walked in and sat a pillow on the chair. He then took the .22 from me, handed me the .44, and then put the pillow over her head and shot her. We both stood there for a moment then I turned and ran. When I got to the car I jumped in and was starting it when Craig jumped in too.

From here I don't remember much till we got to the Dells. Craig later told me he gave me directions on how to get there.

Again I was reminded of an excerpt from recorded sentencing statements; this one from Josh:

Q So you were on your way back to Reedsburg?

A No. We were still heading away, at that point.

Q So you went farther away. Then what did you do?

A We got to the Dells. I switched places with Craig because I had never driven in the city before, and I didn't think that I would be able to handle it and which – we decided that everything was screwed up, you know, and none of that stuff was supposed to happen, and we were going back and so we drove – we were going to get some gas for the car to make it back with, because I believe it had like a half of a tank, at that time, so we didn't know if that would be enough or not. We pulled up at the – some motel or something, couldn't find – figuring out how to open the gas cap on the outside and that got us frustrated. We – I don't know...

– Josh's testimony, Criminal Complaint, State of Wisconsin Circuit Court, Sauk County, pp. 529-30

Once there I told Craig I was going back and after some talk he said he would too, but that he wanted to try and get away with it. I agreed. He bought gas, to burn the car, then drove us back to his home town. He said he knew a good place to burn the car where no one would see it.

Once there Craig and I dumped the gas all over in the car, then I headed off in the direction Craig said to go, in some woods. He then set the car on fire, and at that time a truck stopped. Craig talked to them, then they drove off. I came out of the woods, and we made our way to Craig's house.

Later that night, about 4 hours or so, is when the cops came for Craig. He then gave a statement and told them what happened. They then came for me. The rest is pretty obvious.

I must point out that the time of the crime, when Jackie caught us, to when Craig shot her was very fast, a couple of minutes at best. Also I was quite scared, so I'm sure I've missed a few things that happened, and with so much time that has passed. I apologize for this. But the main stuff is there I believe. Also you can fill in some of the gaps from Craig's story. Between us you'll probably get a pretty complete picture.

As to your second question, for a long time I had no idea how Jackie felt about us, or anything at all. Do to my appeal I didn't get into contact with Jackie until late "99," right before I was sent out of state.

It was when I got in contact with him, not he with me, Jackie adds.

So we were only able to write letters to each other. She did express her "forgiveness" and "love" for us. But it was awhile before I realized what she meant by "love." To be honest I'm not sure I even know now. I believe that she means "love" for your neighbor, as yourself. I believe that for Jackie there the same thing, or very close. So in that sense, she "loves" us because she's forgiven us. That she could forgive us after what we did is nothing short of amazing! I don't think most people could truly do it. I think that I didn't truly believe Jackie had forgiven me until I met her. I expected a lot of things that she might have said, or yelled at me, but she was very kind and forgiving and although she asked some hard questions, I felt a sense of peace of spirit that had been troubling me for many long years! I'll never forgive myself for what I did, but I do look to Jackie for an example of how we all should act towards others! Her sense of, or desire to help others, for nothing in return, not many people are like that, at least not in my dealings.

I've changed a lot since the time of the crime. Jackie, I think, understands better than most that we were kids and that's how we thought and felt, like many teenagers these days, unloved, rejected, lost in a world that doesn't care about us at all. But after that I've had to grow up very fast in here and prison life is definitely not a good place to be when your shaping your mind into adulthood. I was lucky in that I found God early, and have very loving family and friends who helped me stay on the right path! And I think self-discipline; control of my emotions has been a huge impact on who I've become. It's what's kept me on the straight and narrow, which in an environment of crime and unstable emotions that is very hard to do. Not many in here can distance themselves from the dumb stuff, for whatever their reasons may be. It's always easier to go along with the majority. So basically I just do the best I can in the situation I'm in.

I hope this is what you were looking for. If you need more, please let me know and I'll do my best to help you. And thank you for including me in this, and I look forward to reading the book when it's done.

Sincerely,
Josh

Jackie sits shaking her head. *So many lives have changed outside of mine and Craig and Josh's. My two sons. My family. My friends and their families. They didn't know that it affected so many people's lives. You can look at it and you can say, Look how it affected so many people's lives negatively. But I tend to look at the positive. I have gotten to know them.* Jackie puts her hand on her chest then pushes her glasses up, rubbing her eyes. *I have shown him nothing but love. I have gotten to know Josh; I have seen him three times now. I love them as you would love your fellow man. I don't love Craig and Josh with the same love I have for my sons, Derek and Chad. I have to say I love Derek and Chad unequivocally. But I love Craig and Josh as my fellow human beings.* Jackie hooks her thumbs on her blue jean pockets – a task that requires concentration. Her left hand holds her right pocket open while she pushes her lame right thumb into the space. And then she puts her left thumb into her other pocket. And when this is completed, she continues talking. *I realized that my life has changed but I am richer; that is something I hope I am teaching Josh and Craig. They may have tried to kill me but I love them. So many people say,* You are not of your right mind. *They think my brain is all mixed up. It isn't. It isn't.*

No matter what they did. I would like to take Craig out for supper. I would like to take Josh out for a walk. I can't. They are in prison for attempted homicide.

SAUK COUNTY SHERIFF'S DEPARTMENT INTERVIEWS

When I arrived for the sentencing hearing of one of her assailants that June morning, there was a funereal atmosphere in the packed room. But the breaved [sic] Jackie Millar was not in a casket. She was hunched over in the front row, flanked by her two sons, weeping uncontrollably. No one ever expected to see her in person, much less watch her drag herself to the witness stand following the showing of her video to face her assailant.

– Mike O'Connell, The Miracle of Jackie Millar,
The Baraboo Sun. Thursday, April 17, 1997

There were other papers in Sheriff Butch's basement, including transcripts from the interviews conducted with Josh and Craig when they were first arrested after the accident. Below are some excerpts from those papers; information that augments the stories Craig and Josh have sent to Jackie.

Excerpts from sheriff's interview with Craig

Incident title: **Robbery / Attempted Homicide**
Time: **November 5, 1995, 11:53pm**

Interviewer: OK, let's go back to...you're walking out...you said you were looking for a car. What were you going to do with that car?

Craig: Leave....we wanted to leave the state with this car forever, not come back....

Interviewer: What was your intent when you left the house with the gun?

Craig: Just to leave. We...I had no intention of shooting anybody or anything with it. We were just going to leave...

Interviewer: Why did you pick that particular house?

Craig: Because I got sick of walking at that point...

Interviewer: What happened when she got up?

Craig: She came outside and asked if...we needed something...

Interviewer: Then what happened?

Craig: Well, we went inside and I told her to get to get on the ground and...

Interviewer: Did she get on the ground?

Craig: Yeah.

Interviewer: Which room are you in now?

Craig: That living room area...

Interviewer: Laying on the floor now?

Craig: Yeah.

Interviewer: Then what happened?

Craig: I grabbed a pillow and (unclear) her head and...shot her. (unclear)

Interviewer: Why did you do that?

Craig: Because, I don't know, I guess I've seen it in the movies that it muffles the sound and if you kind of wanted to get away you know, without having people find us (unclear). We knew we'd eventually get caught with no way to get out of it and then...I don't know, I guess my mind just started going haywire after that about it...

Interviewer: What was her condition?

Craig: When we left?

Interviewer: Yeah.

Craig: Um, I shot her and her body went limp so I figured I killed her so I...we took off and left. And then from there I just started breaking down...

Interviewer: Why was it necessary to shoot her?

Craig: I don't know. Figured I guess she would have squealed if um, like we stopped her there...we...I was just gonna tie her up and then I don't know...I don't know.

Interviewer: When did you...when did you start...when did you form this line to...to shoot her? When she was laying on the floor? Before that, you weren't thinking of shooting her?

Craig: No, cause we were just going to leave cause she was sleeping and I thought we'd just be able to go without you know her actually having anything to do with it and I was just going to tie her up and then all of a sudden just kind of went blank and we were gone driving the car...

Interviewer: Did you talk about shooting her before you shot her?

Craig: Not really, no. He was...both of us had just having problems and he said he wanted to leave too. Maybe we could get the car to get out of here and head down into the southern states or whatever you want to say...

Interviewer: Describe what the car looks like?

Craig: Ah...I'm sure it's a 95 Honda, a little whatever you call them. It's red. It's got like gray interior and it's like the seats are kind of darkish-lightish gray, not that dark and not like the steering wheel and all the like rubber and plastic and stuff so they're really dark gray, almost like a black. And it...it had like, you know, all really, you know, decent whatever you want to say, radio in it and...[8]

***

*According to psychologist and criminologist Edwin McGargee,
three-quarters of all murders are committed not by overtly aggressive people,
but by the quiet, seemingly well-behaved men who have never found
a safe or appropriate outlet for their aggression.[9]*

***

[8] *...in interviews with police officers who have been involved with shootings, these same details appear again and again: extreme visual clarity, tunnel vision, diminished sound, and the sense that time is slowing down. This is how the human body reacts to extreme stress, and it makes sense. Our mind, faced with a life-threatening situation, drastically limits the range and amount of information that we have to deal with. Sound and memory and broader social understandings are sacrificed in favor of heightened awareness of the threat directly in front of us. Gladwell, Malcolm (2005). Blink: The Power of Thinking Without Thinking. New York: Little, Brown and Co., p. 224.*

[9] Sax, Leonard (2005) *Why Gender Matters: What Parents and Teachers Need to Know About the Emerging Science of Gender Differences.* New York: Broadway Books, p. 64.

*[There was]…ample evidence of [Craig's] good character including…[his]
pastor [who] testified that he was a respectful young man
and very active in church affairs – particularly its youth group…
and…written statements from three other individuals
expressing their disbelief in [Craig's] involvement in the shooting
and explaining that this act was wholly inconsistent
with [his] overall good character.*

*– Court of Appeals Decision of October 1, 1998, State of Wisconsin
(Arguments rejected; original judgment and order affirmed)*

Excerpts from sheriff's interview with Josh

Incident title: Robbery
Time: November 5, 1995, 12:35 am

Interviewer: Who had the gun?
Josh: We both did. We both had our own guns.
Interviewer: You had a gun too?
Josh: Yeah.
Interviewer: What kind of gun did you have?
Josh: I had a .22 caliber.
Interviewer: What does it look like?
Josh: Kind of like a western gun.
Interviewer: OK, and what kind of gun did ah…
Josh: A .44.
Interviewer: Craig had a .44?
Josh: Yeah.
Interviewer: Was that like a automatic or…
Josh: Ah, it's only a six-shot repeater.
Interviewer: OK.
Josh: And we just told her not to move and she didn't and we like took her back in the house and made her lay down in the front room on the floor and then ah, Craig put his gun down and he took my gun, the .22, cause I gave…I wasn't sure if I wanted to shoot her or not. He went in the bedroom and came back out with a pillow and then I was standing there and I was gonna do it at first but…I just didn't…so he took it and then went over there and kind of

looked at me and I just looked at him and kind of shrugged and he just put the pillow up towards the back of her head and shot her. I don't know exactly where he hit her, you know. Couldn't see no blood or nothing. She just kind of laid there and didn't move. A little bit of jerking...I don't know, nerves or something like that...

Interviewer: OK. Why this house?

Josh: No particular reason. We were just walking. We were tired. I pulled a muscle in my calf so...I couldn't walk very fast and we were getting tired. We were just going to try and like steal somebody's car that was just sitting along the road or something but every time we looked there was no keys or nothing or all the doors were locked. We don't know how to hot wire a car or nothing so we decided to just try to get one from somewhere. We were just gonna you know, try and...first we were going to like see if we could get the car you know, (unclear) but I think we just kind of freaked out...

Interviewer: What was the lady saying when she was laying on the floor?

Josh: She just said...um,...when we asked her if anybody else lived there she said no. And then she just said don't hurt me. And we just told her to be quiet and...and then...that's when he came back out...I was...I told her to be quiet cause she asked...she said don't hurt me cause we asked...I asked if there was anyone else in the house and she said no. Said she was divorced or something. I think she said she was divorced...

Interviewer: Did you get any money out of the purse or anything? Out of the lady's purse?

Josh: I think like may be six bucks.

Interviewer: OK. And what'd you use that for? McDonalds or gas?

Josh: No, I think...yeah, think we might have used it at McDonalds...

Craig took the .22 caliber. Granted it had hollow point bullets in it, but I believe he did that so I would survive.

– Jackie

FORGIVENESS? • PAM

We meet a second time with Jackie's sister, Pam. I pull together a list of personality traits attributed to Jackie from our many interviews. I want Pam to respond to which of these characteristics Jackie had as a child and which she may have developed or unleashed since her brain injury. But what I am most interested in is the source of Jackie's forgiveness. Was Pam surprised that Jackie forgave Craig and Josh so quickly, so wholly?

Pam tells us she has joined the Madison Urban Ministry (MUM) *Circle of Support.* This is one of the programs MUM puts on for returning prisoners and their families with the hope of reducing recidivism. As we begin our second conversation, Pam is describing a returning prisoner simulation she was recently a part of at Oakhill Correctional Institution, a minimum security facility near Madison. *These are prisoners who are going to be released in six months. They have to find housing, a job, their parole officer, their AA support group, and build new relationships with their families. Of the eighteen who were supposed to come to my AA table in the simulation, only six came. They are so ill equipped to leave the institution. I decided to join MUM because you can't bitch about the correctional system if you aren't doing something about it.*

I met Craig one year ago. I did it because Jackie asked me to. It was a big step for me because initially I wanted them killed and I am not a violent person. I started crying when I looked at this twenty-six-year-old kid who has been in maximum security prison for ten years. He was hoping to get a job in the kitchen which is a move up from cleaning tables. I asked him about courses and he said he was on the waiting list for Anger Management but it would be five years before he could get in. It was a hard meeting because just looking at him brought up bad memories. I cried. And I ended up feeling sorry for him. It blew me out of the water. We have to rehab these people if we are going to put them in prison. We are not solving anything and are teaching them bad habits. We aren't helping them to rehabilitate. I hadn't thought at all about the prison system before Jack's accident. But my compassion for people in prison is coming out; I am moving from anger to compassion.

Turning to Jackie, Pam says, *I'll never forget the looks on Craig and Josh's faces when they saw you in the court room. Both of them thought you would walk away like people do on TV. They saw your brace and your cane and they were horrified. People don't have a clue what everyone around a victim goes through and how far-reaching it is. I lost one-and-a-half years of my life.*

We begin to talk about the list of personality characteristics with Pam responding to each one:

Strong-headed, strong-willed? Jackie was strong-willed to a point but she is much, much more so now. She was always strong-willed related to anything affecting her kids but in other aspects of her life, no. When we were children, Jackie was the pleaser; the oldest child. She didn't want any of the three of us kids to get into trouble. She would get me crackers when I had the croup in the night to help me stop coughing. She was always the one to take the blame when it was something I had done. She knew she wouldn't get in as much trouble as I would. There is a delightful sisterly moment as Pam and Jackie laugh and tilt their heads together. Pam says, *I was the demon.* Jackie responds, *And I was the mother; I would try to make things OK.*

Shy? Jackie was extremely shy and afraid. In school she had few friends. Family was everything and pleasing family was central. Our parents lined up her first date in high school. She married at 20; the first guy she really knew. She always worked and took care of us kids. Jack was always shy and even as an adult I could bully her and I did.

Trusting? I used to get so angry with you. You trusted everyone. I trusted no one. We had many fights over this. You lived in a fairy tale world. After your divorce, you would hook up with these guys…well, we won't go there. But I just wanted to shake you.

Independent? You were very independent your whole life because you had no one to count on until the Wisconsin Medical Society.

Humorous? Humor wasn't part of our upbringing but it became a way to cope as adults. A way to stay afloat. There has been an impishness since you were hurt, Pam says to Jackie. *We would be walking and I'd lose you and find out you were hiding on me.*

I ask about **restlessness** and Jackie answers this question.

I walk if I'm upset. It is because I can't sit and think about things. Being blind and paralyzed has taken so much away. I want to be as normal as possible.

The next word on the sheet of personality characteristics is **intelligence**. Pam states, *Very intelligent. Always.*

Private? Jackie responds. *I always wanted to have my space. I will have at least one or two feet between me and others. There I am free. That is my space.*

Pam adds, *You don't like people too close because you can't see them.*

Emotional? You showed no emotion as a child or an adult until after your head injury. Then the emotions came out. You'd say, I'm not going to do this no matter what you think! *The psychologist told me to step back and allow you space so you didn't stagnate. I do and what do you do? You walk across John Nolen Drive! You walk across University Avenue! Again and again you gave me heart attacks! Crossing highways!*

Jackie punches Pam in the shoulder, laughing. *I had to take chances. I had to do it myself. There are so many limitations as a disabled person. But I can wear a hat. And I can cross highways. I am not a prisoner.* Turning to Pam again with a provocative smile, *What's* your *answer to that?*

Selfless? Pam ignores Jackie's taunt and we move on to the next characteristic. *Jackie was too selfless. She was always putting others before herself until her brain injury. You became selfish when you were recovering. Dealing with a head injury, a person has to work eight hours a day,* Pam explains to me. *Many times you would cry saying you were too tired to learn any more. But you had to focus on yourself. You had to work so very hard to recover. It took two years before you asked me how I was! That sort of determination is a survival issue for people with brain injuries.*

Compassionate? Jackie responds. *If you are talking about compassion, I think I am. To everybody. I respect everybody. It doesn't matter if they are red, green or yellow, out or incarcerated. I respect them. They are fellow human beings.*

We come up to my central question about forgiveness and I sit lightly waiting to hear this answer. Will I learn more about where forgiveness came from? Where in Jackie? Where in their shared childhoods? Pam speaks.

Forgiving? I was really shocked. Forgive a kid who shot you and then visit him? I thought she was nuts. Jackie was always compassionate and always the peacemaker. She was hard on herself. I know what she was like. But I was beside myself about this forgiveness business. I asked the psychologist what the hell was the matter. I'd tell my family I thought it was the head trauma that made you crazy; like some neurons got mixed up in your brain!

And you weren't forgiving in your rehabilitation. You pulled out feeding tubes until the nurses went crazy and decided just to let you try to feed yourself. You pulled out your catheters again and again. You once threw your shoes at me. There was no forgiveness there! And then the first thing you talked about was, What did I do? *What did YOU do? Dumb head, you did nothing.*

Jackie listens to Pam. She doesn't look at her but turns her head toward her slightly, taking in all of the words. There is silence following the description of forgiveness and I realize I haven't gotten my answer. I still don't know where within Jackie the ability to forgive has come from. Although she will tell me, and has, that she forgave initially so that she could go on with her life, I know there is more to her forgiveness. I have seen it in her actions. She has not only forgiven the boys who attempted to murder her, she has taught them love. She has transformed these boys in ways that might not ever have happened for them. It is the gift beyond comprehension for so many in Jackie's audiences. It is the question that always comes up and there is something that looks like stunned disbelief among many of the people Jackie speaks to.

Jackie turns to Pam and says, simply, *Forgiveness is my present to them.*

And Pam replies, *Yes, I know, you create your life from now on. You have that power.*

FORGIVENESS[10]

◆━━✕━━◆

...without forgiveness, without reconciliation, we have no future.

– Desmond Tutu

◆━━✕━━◆

In one breath, Jackie admits she has no actual memory of the shooting or the subsequent events. In a second breath, she tells me that she forgave the

---

[10] Robert Enright has spent his academic career studying forgiveness. He sees authentic forgiveness as inclusive of, and greater than, the following four ideas:

• Forgiveness is more than simply accepting or tolerating the injustice. It is not about moving on or putting the past behind us; it is about making room for the injurer.

• Forgiveness is not the same as forgetting. A deep injustice is rarely wiped from consciousness.

• Forgiveness is more than ceasing our anger toward the injurer. It is more than taking a boys who shot her the minute the trigger was pulled. Is this an impossible contradiction?

Jackie is explaining, *It just felt right. Forgiveness.*

They were just boys – 15 and 16 years old; they were like my sons.

First to say, I don't like getting shot in my head. But, I would be in a small padded room if I didn't forgive. I wanted to survive so I forgave Craig and Josh. But I don't forget. I will remember until I die that they tried to eliminate me. Most of my audiences don't get me. They think I should hate the boys, I should be scared about them, I should think of ways to get them. Some of the prisoners I talk to tell me they would kill the boys. That is no kind of life for me; no kind of thinking. Forgiveness is, in part, a gift I give myself.

I cannot put myself in the place of the wrongdoers. I cannot understand why the boys attempted to take my life. They were just teenagers that got caught up in the moment. Craig wanted to take back the bullet as soon as he fired the gun. But it can't be taken back.

Meeting the boys has been icing on the cake. I wanted to go on with my life. It took me seeing and writing to them. Meeting the boys was not about closure; it was just a chapter in this journey.

When I met Craig the first time in the prison, I had barely gotten seated when he wanted to tell me he was the one responsible for shooting me. He wanted to tell me that, through tears. He did not do it to boast. He did it for himself, to live with himself. But this I will remember. This I will remember. All I could do was look down at the table. It was as if the person who was telling me he was guilty was my son. I think that started the desire to hug him. I saw him as a human who had made a mistake. He moved me when he told me he shot me. They could say you are nuts, but I got my life back again through talking with Craig. I got back my spirit.

---

neutral stance toward the injurer.
• Forgiveness is more than making ourselves feel good. Forgiveness is a gift to others, not just to self, and the process may lead to psychological healing. The ideal of forgiveness is reconciliation [and, in Jackie's case, her ideal of forgiveness is love].

(Enright, Robert D. & Joanna North (1998). Exploring Forgiveness. Madison: University of Wisconsin Press, pp.44-8.)

I would have forgiven the boys even if they had not been as sorry as they were; even if the boys had said they did not shoot me. But, and people look at me like I'm nuts when I say this, I love them. I love Craig and Josh. I don't know how to hate. I am teaching them. I am angry that they were not taught about love earlier. I am doing it. I am teaching them about love.

I don't know that the boys have forgiven themselves; I think they are too busy with guilt. For instance – Josh was told that I was – I always mix this word up – glad handing – that isn't what I mean. THIS I HATE. I CAN THINK OF THE WORD IN MY BRAIN AND IT WON'T COME OUT. I AM GOING TO THINK OF THIS WORD. That I was too busy thinking how great I was – no, not great. They thought…GRAND STANDSTANDING – awe jeez – GRAND STANDING it. THIS is grand standing? THIS IS GRAND STANDING?? THIS IS GRAND STANDING MY EYES? THIS IS GRAND STANDING MY RIGHT SIDE? Whew. I think, NO IT ISN'T GRAND STANDING what I'm doing when I meet with prisoners and youth. When Josh told me he had heard this, I asked him if he didn't want his letters read or his picture shown at my presentations. And he wrote back and said, I gave you permission to use whatever means. He knows the reasons why I talk to kids and adults.

That hurt my feelings though. How could anyone think I was grand standing?

I ask, *Have you forgiven the boys' parents?*

It is a clash of values…the simplest values. Love. Boundaries. I think I have forgiven the parents. But you'd think that they could teach their boys about right and wrong. I am angry at them. I forgive them but I am angry at them. I feel anger. I feel sadness. But I can forgive them. I would still…but I may be wrong. I think what keeps playing over and over and over in my mind is that the parents were adults and here are their two kids.

If they had come to me and had shown remorse, I think I would feel differently.

The boys have told me they hated everybody because they felt everybody hated them. That is beyond me. I don't comprehend. I asked my younger son to make me understand. And he said he couldn't because he knew about love. He knew about boundaries. That's coming from a kid who had just turned 19; he was two years older than Craig.

I don't know how to hate. I don't hate Craig and Josh's parents. It was said by Craig to a reporter that he learned more about love since the shooting than he did in the first 16 years of his life.

I believe you have two kinds of forgiveness. The forgiveness where you don't want to see them and the forgiveness where you want to see them. In one instance, you want them out of your life and mind. In the other, you bring them to you.

If the parents came forward and said they want to have a meeting, I would go. I am not close-minded about it, but I know I would cry. I look at a person as, Are they sorry? *and* Are they able to be sorry?

So, yes, in one breath, Jackie tells me she has no memory of the shooting or the subsequent events. In a second breath, she tells me that she forgave the boys who shot her the minute the trigger was pulled.

Is this an impossible contradiction?

In the months I have listened to Jackie and heard so many others talk about her I have come to believe.

I believe she forgave the boys immediately when the trigger was pulled. And I believe that Jackie's choice – because of her brain injury – was not initially a conscious decision to forgive. Jackie's forgiveness came innately, instinctively, naturally from her heart, her soul…Jackie forgave.

Jackie forgave because she is Jackie Millar.

OLBRICH GARDENS

Peace is harder to make than war.

– Sammy Weintraub, *11 Days in December*

Jackie and I decide to walk in Madison's Olbrich Gardens one rainy afternoon. For no reason.

Jackie's mix of boldness and shyness stands out in this public place.

The boldness is evident in her continuing willingness to take this adventure – not just in the gardens – but the larger exploration into the accident, her forgiveness, and her subsequent restorative justice work.

We walk along a brick garden path. Jackie reports a nephew said he looks forward to Josh and Craig's release. *I have friends...*, he said. There is a pause and Jackie asks me what the red flower ahead of us is. *A late blooming rose,* I answer, *Like a wild rose that has distinct petals, different than hybrid roses.* She reflects, *My nephew cannot be thinking of me when he talks about hurting Josh and Craig.*

Tall grasses appear to our right. Their seed heads are fully formed and softly bristly. I reach out to touch one and Jackie follows suit. *Soft.*

Jackie sees spots of color and I identify those plants I can both through knowledge and through the informational signs at their bases. We laugh at my pronunciations of the Latin names. *Others would look through my eyes and say,* It isn't so good. *If you were in my line of sight, I'd say,* I don't see you.

I explain to Jackie that I am smashingly beautiful and am so sorry she cannot see me to know that.

Looking at me out of the corner of her eye, she says, *99.9% of the people I talk with tell me they are smashingly good looking. I tell them I am beautiful too but then I remember you can see the truth. On my speaking engagements, the kids ask me how I can talk to such big groups and I tell them,* I pretend you are all blind.

We walk toward the rainforest dome. The entrance has a double door – an area to capture any fleeing residential butterflies and birds. In the space (I later learn such a space is called a sally port in prisons), several children bubble excitedly and are very much underfoot; used to adults walking around them. Jackie shuffles through and around the mix of happy people. I watch but do not interfere, knowing how she prizes her independence.

Inside, it is rainforest hot. Pitcher plant flowers are hanging in our pathway. I hold one taut flower out for Jackie to touch. She does. Down the walkway is another plant with many knobs on the leaves. I explain that this leaf has Braille on it and she reaches out, willingly. We both know she doesn't read Braille.

Later, as we get in the car to head home, Jackie asks me to drop her off at

Quiznos in Hilldale Mall. I do, then look back to see her standing alone on the busy sidewalk, straw hat on her head, white cane with its red bottom in her hand. She looks left; right. So often I have thought that, as an olding woman, I am invisible in this world. Jackie is too. She shifts her weight from foot to foot. Single people pass. Families pass. All are unaware of this woman who has made herself remarkable in response to circumstances beyond her control. No one offers help. No one even looks at her. And Jackie's basic shyness seems to have returned. She does not approach anyone. I drive away wondering if she will get a sandwich.

RESTORATIVE JUSTICE[11]

Jackie's work is to talk with people about choices and love.
She meets with youth in the juvenile justice system,
with adult prisoners from jails to maximum prisons, with lawyers,
District Attorneys, police officers, guards, judges, and students.

*She's an active fighter in the national restorative justice movement,
which tries to elevate the role – and consider the needs
– of crime victims and the community
in a process that's often focused strictly on offenders
and law enforcement professionals.*

– Steven Walters[12]

Jackie lives restorative justice.

I talk to hardened criminals. I have hugged men who have killed someone, raped someone, burned something. I respect them. I love them as fellow human beings. It is so easy to love them.

What do you see in these men? I ask.

---

[11] Mark Umbreit directs the University of Minnesota Center for Restorative Justice and Peacemaking. From their website:
The process of victim offender mediation or conferencing has been found to be most effective when the following concerns are addressed:

I see a child inside. I see my sons. They could have been my sons. My sons would cringe at my saying this; don't tell them. I am not afraid; I go into a prison softly. I respect the inmates and I think they are caught off guard. They don't know what to do with me. I shake their hands. I touch them.

I think that I am the most positive person I know. If there is a way to be positive, I find it. I should be deathly afraid of all inmates. They start out being so big, so bad and so bold. I am not afraid. When I am there in the prisons, I feel at peace. I know the guards are watchful but I am not afraid because the inmates won't hurt me. I have paid my dues. The inmates protect me.

One man tried to ask me a question but couldn't because of his tears. I touched his hand and it made the crying worse. I said, I don't want your pity. *Another man stood and said,* It isn't pity, it's our...like admiration, our respect...for you.

All I have to do is teach everyone to love each other. What a good world we would have. What a lot of work to do.

- *Victim-sensitive procedures that are respectful and offer choices.*
- *Respectful treatment of those who commit criminal acts.*
- *Voluntary participation by all parties.*
- *Encouragement of family members or other support people to participate in the process, but respecting the choice of victim and offender if they prefer to meet one-on-one.*
- *In-person preparation of the involved parties before they meet each other.*
- *Use of a style of mediation that is "dialogue driven" not "settlement driven".*
- *Flexibility, so that the process can be adapted to the specific needs and cultural context of the parties.*
- *Avoidance of a "one size fits all" approach that assumes either a small one-on-one session or a larger group session with many support people is always best for all people and anchoring this decision in the expressed needs of the victim and offender.*

www.restorativejustice.org/resources/leading/umbreit

[12] *Journal Sentinel Newspaper,* Sunday, March 21, 1999, p. 1.
In Walters' article, Mark Umbreit is quoted as saying, Wisconsin is one of a growing number of states that is trying to make statewide initiatives on behalf of restorative justice.

Jackie speaks to students as well as prisoners.
She receives hundreds of letters. Here is one:

Dear Jackie,
Thank you for coming to our school to talk to us, your story is really inspiring.
I am religious too, I always wear a blessed cross around my neck.
I have had it since I was in the 2ⁿᵈ grade. I got it for my first communion.
It has always kept me safe. I want to give it to you.
Sincerely, M

– 7ᵗʰ grader at Horicon Marsh Middle School
(Her small cross and chain are taped to the back of her letter)

DANE COUNTY JUVENILE JAIL • A SPRING TALK

Eleven boys and three girls file into the small room and sit on institutional plastic chairs. There are no windows and the only sound is the air conditioner blower. They arrange themselves by gender and age, but not race. Eight are African American, far more than would be present if the group reflected local county demographics. Their clothes are jail issue: baggy ecru or forest green cotton outfits that most closely resemble cheap pajamas. For many, the pant legs are rolled up several times to allow them to walk without tripping. All wear rubber jail-issue sandals. No one could run in those shoes, I think to myself.

There is wiggling. A guard reassures the youth they won't have to touch Jackie's head. He says to us, *The kids are freaking out about this.* A child blurts out, *You got shot in the head? THAT would hurt!*

I remember Jackie talking about incarcerated *babies.* Some of these kids look like they are 10 years old. Jackie asks a question and a mixed-race boy with fresh, whiskerless cheeks knows the answer. He has heard Jackie speak before in this same place. His hands have no wrinkles. His fingernails are long.

Jackie continues to talk and there is silence. Wiggling stops. All eyes are on her as she walks back and forth. Her right foot is dragging; her right hand is curled and her arm looks heavy and ineffectual. Her words linger in the air: *28 lines in me, 2 shunts in my head...*

Earlier Jackie had explained to me, *I touch the youth. I used to think I touched them because of what had happened to me but now I think it is because they see I give them respect. They give it to me in return. It is so hard for me to put it into words.*

You may ask any questions of me, except one, and that is, What is my weight. That is between me and God. There is silence; it is an adult joke.

One of the boys asks the first question. *What does hit-and-miss mean?*

Jackie responds. *I will remember things one day and not the next.*

Another boy. Another question. *Does a hollow point bullet explode when it goes in?*

Yes. I have seven bullet fragments in my brain. I have a CAT *scan every 9 to 12 months. If the bullet fragments move I could die or become a vegetable.*

What kind of vegetable? The question is asked seriously. The child does not know the term. Older, wiser kids chuckle but Jackie answers sincerely.

It means I would not be able to speak and would just lie there.

Why did you hug the boy who shot you?

Because I am a mother. Jackie pauses. *You look at me incredulous. I am a mother. I am a mother first. Mothers love.*

The boy who asked the question stares. Incredulous is exactly the right description. I sense he wants to ask more but the other children are present. Slowly he sinks in his chair and though the questions continue to come from the other kids, he is clearly still thinking about Jackie's statement. A mother? He pulls his sweatshirt up over his mouth and nose and sits, staring.

Jackie stops the questions and asks the kids to tell her their ages and why they are in the juvenile jail. She clarifies. *If you don't want to tell me why you are here, you may pass.*

I think about the reality that Wisconsin youth can "benefit" from incarceration. Those who may not have engaged parents or access to finances can receive state-supported mental health counseling or alcohol/drug abuse treatment. Often the crime that provides that access is *fighting*.

Most of the children respond with their age and their offense:
16 – battery, a fight
15 – pass
16 – fighting
15 – running away from drug treatment
16 – running away
13 – pass
14 – pass
15 – running away from the shelter
13 – pass
12 – fighting
10 – pass
14 – fighting

The youth begin to fidget. They move into defensive postures with arms and legs crossed. Some slouch in their chairs. The supervisor cautions them to sit up. Two leave the room.

A boy in the back row is asked to read a letter Jackie has received from an adult prisoner in Minnesota. The boy stands and takes the letter. His hands shake. He reads five words in a slow monotone, staccato pattern but stumbles over the sixth word. Jackie has to help him. The word is *society. You cared about us who society feels are worthless,* the prisoner had written.

More comments or questions, Jackie asks.

Three youth speak in succession:

It is sad.

I feel bad.

Take the bus.

Jackie laughs out loud. The child is not trying to be funny; he covers his head with his sweatshirt.

An older youth says, *I think about how easy I have got it compared to you. There is no comparison. I would like to hug you.*

And he does. He walks to the front of the room and, in front of other youth, he hugs Jackie. The group applauds.

Dennis comes to the door. He is the director of this program. His huge body fills the doorway. He rests with one hand on top of the door frame, leaning in. A child squeezes past and Dennis ruffles his hair in a fatherly way. He begins, *Jackie has been coming here for at least three years. She comes once a month. If you don't learn from Jackie, you won't learn. This is real life. This isn't TV. Jackie is a blessing. She can reach people like yourselves. Think about this during Reflection. You still have the opportunity to make changes. That is why Jackie comes here — you still have got opportunities. You can say I don't want to have my life taken away and be in prison for 40 or 50 years.*

The group is awkwardly, adolescently quiet. The mixed-race, whiskerless boy stands and asks if he may come up. He gives Jackie a long, long hug. She pulls him in close. Because I am near them, I can hear what he says to her. *You really touched me this time,* he whispers. *You really touched me.*

As I leave the City-County Building and walk into the bright June sunshine, I feel heavy. Those children should be playing on skateboards. They should be lying in the grass watching bugs. They should be tumbling together like puppies, not caged on the darkened third floor of a downtown institutional building. I hope they heard Jackie's story.

A SECURED JUVENILE CORRECTION FACILITY • A FALL TALK

...For more times than can be recollected, Jackie has made
[a] noticeable difference for individual participants that we,
as facilitators, have really struggled with.
This is a crucial observation when you realize that these youth...
have created many victims; on average 25 victims for each crime.

— Facilitator, Victim Impact Program

I arrive 30 minutes early to meet Jackie and her aide at the correctional boy's school, glad I have allotted the extra time. MapQuest directions have once again led me astray so I have seen overly much of this woodland area. The leaves are fallen and the evergreens and pines stand distinctively in the muted landscape with their shades of dark green to black. The location could be a camp or a park. The school sits high on a hill. My mother, an artist, once told me that the further away something is in a painting, the lighter the color. That truth is evident as I look at the distant ridges, progressively lighter in hue. To my back – as I sit in my car waiting – are fences. I am not good at estimating heights, but they could be 16 feet tall. At the top are triple rows of coiled razor wire. The morning dew on the silver wire shimmers in an ordered design. I watch groups of small, white-winged migrating birds flying and landing and flying again in unison as if their flight is choreographed and set to music. The beauty of this place belies the troubled youth who reside here.

Jackie arrives and is escorted in. There are no screening delays; the staff knows her from previous visits. We are driven to a classroom inside the fenced area.

The boys file in and obediently move the chairs into a horseshoe shape as instructed by their teacher.

Nametags, gentlemen, one instructor says. Each nametag is positioned on the floor in front of the youth.

They are watching Jackie as she walks into the room. Sly looks, out of the corners of their eyes. Curious and hesitant.

Push your chairs back, an instructor barks.

Guest speaker today is Ms. Millar.

Jackie walks slowly into the center of the circle.

I want you to watch this two-minute tape. It does a much better job of introducing me than anybody else.

The boys intently watch the video showing John's house and the nearby

Christmas tree farm. His house is where the shooting occurred. They see the ceremony done there for Jackie after the accident. Her sons, Chad and Derek, are pictured.

As they watch the video, I watch the boys. There are 15 young men in the room. There is no emotion on their faces.

I am Jackie Millar. I was shot in the back of my head and left to die...

All the boys have their hands folded in front of them. A few lean forward.

There stood a .22 caliber and a .44 magnum staring me in the face...

Bright colored light comes in the high windows in the back of the room. The rainbow of colors reflects off the painted dull white cinder block walls. A hand-written sign is posted on the wall: *Offender MUST understand victims side before they can be healed.*

Jackie continues speaking, *I must have tried getting up and getting help. I didn't make it. I fell back down. About how much time do you think there was between when they shot me until when my friend returned?*

A boy offers, *Three hours?*

Jackie counters, *No.*

Thirty minutes? No.

Ten minutes? No, but you are close. 15 minutes...

There is no movement in the room.

The paramedics know I have been shot execution-style. They know one other thing. They know I will be dead by morning...

Jackie walks around and around a small table in the center of the classroom space. There are three photos on the table. The phone rings. One boy is called out of the room. He leaves and some are distracted by the movement.

Several of the boys watch Jackie's foot curl in as she continues her walking and speaking.

They told my sons I only had a 2% chance of making it. They listened to that for two weeks. Then my sons listened to, They might as well get me a room inside a nursing home because I will be a vegetable – or non-existent person – for the rest of my life.

The picture of Jackie and her sons is passing from hand to hand around the circle. Jackie's functional left hand clenches and unclenches as she walks and continues talking.

The boys that did it to me and they were just boys… Your age? Jackie points.

17.

Yours?

15.

Attempted first-degree homicide. They were found guilty…

Some kids shift in their chairs. There is full attention in the room.

The shooter of me, his name is Craig. He was 16 years old. He received 80 years in adult prison. He is eligible to get out when he is 36. WHEN DO I RECEIVE MY PAROLE? WHEN WILL I BE ABLE TO SEE EVERYTHING THAT IS AROUND ME? WHEN WILL I USE THE RIGHT SIDE OF MY BODY AGAIN? NEVER. NEVER.

Josh. He was sweating bullets because he was about to meet the woman he tried to eliminate…

A letter written by Josh is handed to the boy who quickly volunteered to read it. The boy is easily six feet tall. He reads with some hesitation, but relatively well. He wears a mustache and goatee. Like the other boys, he is wearing black shoes with Velcro closings. Jackie stands and listens, correcting some of the words being read. She places her right hand in her jean pocket, forcing the stiff, uncooperative fingers.

After the reading, Jackie commands, *I would like you, you, you, you and you to come up.*

The boys look at their instructors for approval, then stand and file towards Jackie as a group. She turns her back to them and says, *Touch, in between my fingers.* They touch quickly, gingerly.

She announces, *They touched my bullet wound...*

One of the boys who touched Jackie's head pulls his white shirt over his nose and wipes his eyes. He sits bent to the left. He silently touches his eyes again. He wipes his nose. He leans further to the side.

Another boy awkwardly and rapidly brushes his eyes with the back of his hand.

I will answer any questions except about my weight. Questions, comments. I know you have some.

Do you know why they did it?

They thought it was the only way to keep me from being an eye witness.

Do you have sex?

Jackie is embarrassed, hesitates then replies, *Now there are two questions I will not answer and one of them is about my weight.* There is uncomfortable laugher from the audience.

How did the boys get caught?

They were caught because — one of the boys, it is Craig — he had just shaved his head. People noticed him.

Do you live in a nursing home?

No, I have my own apartment and I live in it all by myself.

What do you feel towards them?

You will either say hmm or you will say I'm nuts, but I love them. I love them but

I am angry that they tried to kill me.

Does the bullet in your brain affect how you dream?

My long-term and short-term memory…to dream I would have to have recall. I don't have that. That was taken away from me. One day I will remember, the next day it is gone.

Do you still see your kids?

Yes. One lives in Iowa with his wife and two little girls. The other one lives in Pittsburgh.

What did your sons feel about the situation?

When they heard I had been shot, they had wished that the boys who did it could burn in hell. Burn in hell. My kids had to come home from college and had to go to my house and find my will and come up to the hospital and say goodbye to me.

Do you still have contact with Josh and Craig?

I see them once a year. I can write to them numerous times; they can write to me numerous times.

Will you have contact with them when they get released?

Yes. I think so, but they will probably get released when they are in their 50s.

You were in the hospital for how long? Did you have to pay for the bills?

How much did you think it cost?

Boys guess, *$75,000. $100,000.*

More than that. It cost me more than $500,000, not including the months in rehabilitation. I had excellent insurance, so I only had to pay the first $100.

Do you work now? Do you have a job?

I go around talking to youth, adults. I talk about forgiveness; I talk about choices; I talk about love. I talk for nothing. It is my gift to talk. I think I have a story to tell.

Do you have flashbacks from that day?

I don't think I do but I might have flashbacks. I don't remember. I am scared at night. I am scared but I don't want to let my fears rule.

Are you scared of guns now?

Not so much guns, Jackie replies. *I believe that it is choices I am scared of. I am not scared of guns.*

How do you manage to live by yourself after this experience?

It took a year after the incident. I believe in God. I know that my kids love me and I have this sense of humor that it…I can laugh, I can laugh. I think I laugh because I don't want to cry.

Do you still have memories from when you were growing up?

Some. Like I will remember something one day and the next day it is gone. I remember a lot from pictures.

After the accident, did you remember your sons?

I didn't remember them for weeks and suddenly I remembered and when they walked into my room at the hospital, I just had this grin on my face, like oh boy, I was going to see my sons. But before then I didn't know anybody.

Your memory is bad. Do you take notes?

If I took notes it would be useless because I can't see that good. My family and friends just know that I will lose a memory and we deal with that.

Is that Josh's picture right there?

That is Craig.

Jackie walks around the circle holding Craig's picture.

He is standing with a friend. It was taken at Green Bay Prison.

Jackie picks up the second picture sitting in a frame on the center table and again walks around the room showing it.

This is Josh, the one in the middle. He is surrounded by his brother and sister. It was taken at Oklahoma Prison; we have too many Wisconsin inmates; we have to ship them out of state.

I would like to start here, Jackie points to the youth on her left. *You give me your age and why you are here.*

One young man talks about stealing a car and Jackie asks rhetorically,

What would you have done if the operator would have tried to stop you?

Another inmate tells her his crime was armed robbery and she asks,

What would have happened if you had used the weapon and the person died? What would you be charged with?

Murder.

Murder. First-degree murder.

And then.

Why did you steal a car?

I have no idea.

The litany continues: age and crime.

Many of your charges were done with guns. Why did you have guns? Jackie asks and there is a flurry of replies from the boys.

For protection.

To make me look good.

There is no reason to have one.

Jeez. I am the perfect example. You DON'T need guns. Jackie is crying as she speaks. *They told me to lie down on the living room floor. They then took the gun …the .22 pistol. It had in it hollow point bullets. Who knows what they are?* Everyone in the room raises their hands.

Jeez! Everybody!

Jackie tests the boys. *What are hollow point bullets? When they hit an object, like my head, what do they do?*

They answer in unison: *They break up. They break up and do their damage.*

I had to lie in a hospital in a coma. My sons were there holding my hands. I did not know. I think of your reasons for having guns. To look good? You thought it would be fun? You thought you needed it? I don't have any knowledge from two weeks before the incident until six weeks later.

There is discomfort in the room now. Shuffling. Lip licking.

Jackie talks about her sons' experiences. *My sons held my hand. They cried.*

Jackie cries. The tears are not staged; could not be. My sense is that her disappointment, her horror, is not with these boys but with a society that makes them think they need guns to look good; to be cool.

I am a pacifist. That means that everyone loves one another. She puts her hand to her head. *I found out everyone doesn't love one another.*

Jackie points from one boy to another. *I love. I love you. I love you. I don't like what you have done. That is my right. But I love you. I love Craig and Josh. I don't like what they did. I would be the first person to say it.* The moment is dramatic. Silence follows.

Craig, the shooter of me; he wrote me a letter that I got yesterday. He asked if my sons would accept a letter from him. He asked the question if they would write to him. How would you answer that? Jackie points into the audience.

I don't know.

No.

Derek, he is my oldest. I think he would accept a letter from Craig. But I don't know if he would write him back.

Shuffling in the chairs. Nearly all the boys are leaning forward now. I am struck by how well Jackie modifies her presentation to accommodate the age and experiences of her audience. Subtle changes. Different parts of the presentation are amplified for different audiences. She is a pro. I have seen tears on the cheeks of people she talks with; people from age ten to seventy.

I have a poem that was written by my older son, Derek. [See page 157] *I would like one of you to read it, please.* The *please* in Jackie's sentence comes at an absolutely critical time in this conversation. It is a sign of respect for the boys. It is an honoring of the capacities, the potential these young men have to do good in the future.

A boy who has had trouble asking questions through his tears offers to read. Now all the boys are leaning forward, arms resting on knees. Some hang their heads. They have been here for one hour. Are they listening carefully? Are they tired? Are they emotionally overloaded? I do not think they are bored.

Question? Comment? Jackie continues.

How did your sons feel when you went to see Craig and Josh?

They thought I was nuts. But they watched me. They listened to me.

Do you have trouble moving your legs at times?

The right leg hangs behind. It does nothing. I can't go running. I can't walk fast.

I wondered about Craig. I asked him three questions in the mail. Which one of you will read this?

A Latino boy stands, slim and lanky, and reads the letter from Craig. He struggles over some words. His hands are steady. His shoulders are rounded, the sleeves of his gray shirt hang to his elbows and thin, boy arms, extend from the jail issue clothing.

There is some stretching and leaning back now, 1 hour and 15 minutes into the program. But there is ease in the room, trust. The rapid-fire questions get more and more personal and Jackie answers easily, openly.

Do you ever forget Craig and Josh?

It is through constant, constant talks with the sheriff's office, the DA, my sister, my kids – they have ingrained in me who the boys are. Sometimes I have – and I want to die every time I do it – I have accidentally called my son Chad, Craig. They both begin with "C." He knew he couldn't get mad at me but he felt badly for himself. But forget them? For the most part, no. There are times I have to stop and think about their names. But forget about them, no.

Can you draw?

I draw with my mind. But I can't draw. It is with my left hand that isn't so good. I shake from the anti-seizure medication I am on.

So if you get poked in your right eye, will you die?

Jackie nods. *The bullet fragments are still in me. They could shift and I could die.*

How do you feel?

I am a miracle. It is a miracle that I am here. Doctors and nurses called me a miracle. My sons call me a miracle. They are 32 and 30 years old now. How are they the ages they are when I am only 35? They said, medical marvel. I cannot tell if the boys get the joke or not; they move on with their focused questions.

Do you have trouble remembering your own name?

Not my own name. I just say it slowly. My address, I say it slowly. It is frustrating to me.

How does it feel to go around to prisons and talk?

Prisons? I like them. I am going to Minnesota prisons in a few weeks. I will be there five days and visit Stillwater (maximum), Lino Lakes (medium), Moose Lake and Willow River (minimum), Faribault (medium), and Oak Park Hill (maximum). I think it is good because for some reason they will see their victims through my eyes. I like coming here. I like meeting you.

Do you still have fun?

Jackie reflects, *I am at peace. I walk a lot. But fun? Fun was a thing I could have before the accident. Now that word is gone from my vocabulary.*

How long did it take you to learn to speak again?

It took nine months to one year. When I was out of my coma, I was a two-year-old child in every sense of the word. And now, I have a tape for you to watch.

The boys turn to the TV sets, even more interested now. They hear *Jackie's Song* and see pictures of Craig and Josh's sentencing hearings.

Questions? Comments?

It sounds like that song was written just for you.

It was. I have a friend who is a record producer. He wrote that song after he heard I had been shot. He had it produced. It was my song.

Do you enjoy listening to music?

All kinds.

I think that song is very beautiful.

I have something that I wrote – a pamphlet. It has my letter and Craig and Josh's letters and the words to the song in it. It is something that I hope you take back and read. I know…I know that you are our future. You have our future in your hands. I think that what Craig and Josh did is horrible and it is not for you. However, they have thrown away their whole young adult life. They will get out of prison when they are middle-aged men. You have to think, to think about each and every choice you have got. If they could, if Craig and Josh could, they wouldn't have shot me. It is that simple. I love each and every one of you. I want only the best things in life for you. But you have to want them too.

May I give you a hug? A young man asks haltingly.

Yes you may, Jackie replies.

Peace.

And loud applause follows.

The questions these youth have asked are generally practical ones. They want the details of the crime and want to more fully understand Jackie's abilities and disabilities. They want to know more about their peers in the story: Derek, Chad, Craig and Josh.

Their inquiries are different than those asked by the adults whose questions are more relational and philosophical. The adult inmates ask spiritual questions. They ask for advice and insights from being given a second chance at life. They ask about Jackie's ability to forgive and her sense of peace.

On my trips to a secured juvenile correctional facility,
I ask the boys how old they are and why they are there.
Once – one kid – he hesitated.
He was obviously older than the rest
and I knew he had to have done something horrible.
He had murdered someone when he was much younger
in a fit of anger when they were both drunk.

I said, May I ask you one question?
Please don't ask me why, *he replied.*
No, not that. I want to know if I can give you a hug.
I did and he kept telling me how glad he was that I was alive.
They are just babies. Babies.

– Jackie

MOOSE LAKE PRISON, MINNESOTA · A WINTER TALK

Jackie and I arrived at the aged prison 45 minutes early to allow time for getting through security. As we wait, I hear her humming aloud; she says she has nervous energy. This is the last of five days of speaking to adult inmates as part of Minnesota's Restorative Justice Program.

We sign in, have our drivers' licenses checked, and then held. We get stamped on the backs of our left hands with an ink that can only be read under blue light. Nate meets us and escorts us through a double door area. On the first of the two doors is a sign reading, *No more than 6 individuals at a time in sally port.* We move easily, past prisoners who are sweeping the hallways. We enter a large room with a wall of windows. Outside the windows, 20 feet away, is the now familiar coiled razor wire. In the room, chairs are set up in a very large circle, two and sometimes three deep. Prisoners file in slowly, checking in at a table. They are ordinary-looking men, nearly all Caucasian in this northern Minnesota facility.

One man has given quiet gang handshakes to two others as they have come in – a handshake I learned about in a recent workshop.

Welcome to our third and final restorative justice program this week. Jackie is here to speak to you from the heart, Nate says.

Applause.

Men continue to file, no, shuffle in slowly.

One of the tapes is played showing evening news stories about Jackie's shooting.

I am Jackie Millar. I was shot in the back of my head and left to die. I went to a friend's house…

More men are coming into the room. All the seats are filling up. The men range in age from about 18 to 60 or more.

They put the gun to my head and pulled the trigger…

Many, but not all, eyes are watching Jackie. The men aren't fully engaged yet.

Some are watching me type; others are watching the men still coming into the room. There are two open seats in the front row. They fill.

Jackie is using her white cane this morning. She has on her red shoes.

More men are coming in. Chairs are pulled away from the walls to accommodate those continuing to file in. They come in quietly, deferentially.

They know I will be dead by morning…

The men are increasingly attentive.

It takes an hour and fifteen minutes to drive between Madison and Reedsburg. By Medivac helicopter, it takes just fifteen minutes. I always wanted to ride in a helicopter but preferably awake. One out of two isn't bad.

There are a few snickers, but mostly quiet.

Jackie takes the picture of her sons and holds it out. *They told my two sons I have a 2% chance of living.* Emotion is increasing in Jackie's talk. There is some visible discomfort in the room. Some toe tapping, some averted eyes.

Attempted first-degree homicide.

Outside of the room I see three prisoners in blue winter coats, walking around the fenced yard. They wear bright orange stocking caps. It is deer hunting season outside the walls.

When do I receive my parole? When can I see everything that is around me? When can I use anything on my right side? Never. Never…

A quarter of the men are leaning forward, hands on knees.

There was one thing additional I wanted from Craig. You guess.

Inmates respond.

Why?

A hug…

Who said hug?

I heard your story three years ago; this from the man who offered the gang handshakes.

Jackie acknowledges him and goes on. *I wanted a hug and he agreed and we hugged long and hard.*

The men in the orange caps pass by the outside window again as they walk the circle; the yard. Inside, there is growing silence in the room. Jackie picks up Craig's letter.

I want one of you to read it. I know you can read; I think one of you can read my letter or I can choose one of you.

Laughter in room. A man, about thirty years old, reads aloud. His arms are on his knees, the letter held between them. He is misreading some of the words – *severely for seriously.* He volunteered to read. He reads word by word rather than sentence by sentence. Is he comprehending what he is reading? Why did he volunteer to read this aloud to his peers? It is powerful to have him reading in this way; there is attentive listening in the group. He is now stammering and adding some *ums.* He is on page one of two. He runs his thumb along under the words.

As the reading continues, I read a poster on the far wall. *When you stumble and fall, get up.* I think of a quote I recently saw in a college textbook, *Fall seven times, get up eight.* Same message. Different context.

From one of Craig's letters, the words hang in the room. *You in the audience are the future. Learn from the mistakes… Please listen to Jackie. Listen to the strength to forgive. Listen to how she took my mistakes and turned them into a blessing for all of you. Someday someone may forgive you for what you have done.*

Jackie takes the letter back and slowly folds it. She says, *Questions? Comments?*

Some people would say you have had a second chance in life. Are there things you are doing that you wanted to do and never done, now that you have a second chance?

I have visited prisons and I have found out that you all are just human beings that made a horrible decision.

One man nods, says, *Amen.*

Personally I am really sad that they made this poor choice to shoot you and I don't think it was a mistake, I think that it was a poor choice. I was sad to hear in the letter that they felt it was a mistake. I look at you in admiration because you have taken this bad event and turned it into something positive for yourself and others.

Pausing and looking down, Jackie adds, *I have been to hell and back. So have my children. But I lived. I think it was a poor decision that they made. They are human beings. They, Craig and Josh, had been – this is a word that is hard for me to remember – but they were shocked that someone would walk through that door when they were stealing my car. They were not in their right mind. I met them. I met them. That is hard, hard to understand.*

The men are not shy. Their comments come rapidly.

I'd like to thank you for coming and sharing your story. This last couple of days I have been inspired by people who are sharing their stories. I get inspiration from the stories; I think of the people I have hurt and the secondary people I have hurt. I don't want to do that again. This statement comes from the man who had heard Jackie's presentation before; the one who gave the gang greeting to other inmates.

Were they on drugs or alcohol when they did this?

No, they were clean.

I want to thank you. I want to think about the empathy I have listening to you. But the screaming inside my head is that I'd want them dead.

Jackie laughs. *That doesn't bring back the person. I died. I died that day, November 4th. It doesn't bring me back. An eye for an eye and soon we are all blind. That is what Gandhi said and I believe it. You kill someone for what they have done to you and it doesn't make sense. It doesn't make sense.*

Do you have a sense of peace? I've heard a person's life flashes before their eyes before death.

Yes. I am happy I get to wake up. That to me is peace. I had a sense of peace. Just to show you how much peace I had before the accident, I was telling the boys not to steal my car; I had payments still due.

Laughter.

I got to say that your smile comes from the inside out. It is beautiful.

Thank you, Jackie replies easily. *I say I am healed from my heart; from the inside.*

I hear whispered *Amens* from around the room.

I am just wondering, from the moment you were shot and you came out of the coma, do you remember anything? A will to survive? Making peace with your maker?

I had a talk with God and he told me to speak. I said, sure. To whom? To the people out there. And I have been talking for, it will be ten years. Eleven years I have been living.

Since you have been going to see Craig, has he been making changes in his life? Does he teach what he is learning to others? Do they have restorative justice programs in Wisconsin?

Yes, Wisconsin has a kind of restorative justice. They are reluctant to have meetings with the perpetrators. I've met both of the boys. I found out they are not monsters. They are not animals. They are not.

Do you feel imprisoned?

I am in prison in my body. I can't drive. If I drove, I would drive on the cement, on the grass, in buildings, in lakes. Oh boy! No one else would drive their car when I drove. I can't drive. I did everything I could do before the accident. After the accident, I am still the mother of two sons, but everything else has been taken away from me.

Jackie, you and my Mom could talk. Mom is 84, can't drive any more because of the arthritis in her back and hips, and she has this monstrous magnifier for reading. But she has such joy, such forgiveness, such an open heart.

Jackie, you might have lost some things in life. But who you are today – sharing your life – is good. You have humor, radiance, and heart and you are sharing your story so others will stop and think.

Thank you, Jackie accepts the compliments gracefully.

How did what happened to you affect your social life, your friends?

Some of my friends couldn't handle it and they moved away, they moved on. I look at it simply as I've gotten new friends. I have gotten new friends that are here to stay.

It happened at your friend's house. How does your friend deal with that?

John has guilt. I can't help him with the guilt. He has to do that all himself.

I have a poem. My oldest son, Derek, he wrote a poem on the 10th year anniversary of the accident and I would like one of you to read it.

I'll read it. A tall black man stands. He reads expressively and easily. His voice sounds like music, a song. He reads with emotion and passion. Heads turn. Many are leaning forward. The inmates applaud, spontaneously, when he finishes.

You have already faced one of the biggest fears in life. I was going to ask you what is your biggest happiness but I think that poem covered it.

Jackie nods. *My biggest fear now is that the boys and girls, men and women, won't listen to me. Won't listen and take heart that they have choices – they have got to think about them. That is my greatest fear.*

Do you find it easier to see through all the crap; to see through the bullshit? To see people?

People say one thing and do another. I think that if I talk from my heart, you will not always do the right thing but you will think about it, I hope.

I want to thank you for coming because to actually see the impact that some decisions make is different than reading about them. You have given me a life lesson that I can show my kids and the repercussions behind our decisions. I will continue to pray for you. I hope you continue to share.

And another inmate adds, *I was wondering, in that letter it sounded like Craig was comparing what he did to you to being late for work. Does he understand the magnitude of what he did to you?*

He understands what he has done. One time I told him my joke – the joke I told you about having dinner with my sister and chewing the paper cup. He didn't laugh. All he did was look down. Later on I wondered about it and asked. He said he couldn't laugh. He had shot me. He couldn't laugh.

One thing I noticed, especially here in prison, is how men complain about the time they got. Hearing your story as well as the others, I realized that my sentence may not have been hard enough if you look at it that way. I've made some very poor decisions in my life. I know I have hurt a lot of people in my day. I feel ashamed that when I first came to prison I felt I got a raw deal. I had to come to terms with the fact that, like you said, your sentence is a life sentence. Whatever we have done, it affects everyone's lives, forever. To recognize that my choices have that effect on others is embarrassing for me to say. Now I see that the time I got was something needed. I can't make up for what I've done but I feel sad about it.

Jackie responds to the inmate's admission, *I look at each of you and I know you have prison time. But so do I, a victim. You don't think I would give anything to ride a bike, to run, to drive a car, to see where I am going? I was just about killed. But you, you know, you have to serve time. I don't know what you did or how many years it is, but you have time. I have time. I can't hold my grandchildren. I would love to hold my grandchildren. I would love to go through a forest and know where I was going. I could go through a green forest; but I wouldn't know where I was going. I would love to stand out and see the sun go down. I don't. I am sorry that you have to serve your time, but so do I.*

With all that you have lost, don't you think you have gained more than a lot of other people have?

Certainly. I know *that I am* alive.

What was the first time you spoke like?

I did so ten years ago. I spoke rather haltingly. More so than I do now — a lot more. I thought then it sounded beautiful! Today I think I talk beautiful. There was one kid who made fun of me — the way I talk. When I could, I said to him, I talk halt-ingly because of them shooting me. *He said he didn't make fun of me and his friend by him said,* Yes you did. You made fun of her. *Some people will make fun of me. Some will stop and stare. All I do is go right on ahead. It is something I do.*

Have you ever thought about writing a book about inspiration and hope for people?

For ten-and-a-half years, the answer was no. My sons had to go through it once, but after ten-and-a-half years they came to me and told me, yes. I am writing a book with Judy, her. Jackie points toward me. *A book that is taking its time. But she is writing it; I am saying it.*

Jackie has one last paper to be read. She explains that for a while she worked at a maximum security facility. *I used to walk in the yard between where the men are housed and where they go to school or to the doctor. One of the men was watch-ing me and he wrote this.*

An inmate volunteers to read another inmate's words.

A victim or an angel

I sat and watched you pass by my prison cell,
With such a joyous smile until it was hard to tell.
I looked to see if you had any pain that was hid somewhere
Deep inside, but to my surprise, there was no pain there.
I who have left so many victims in my past, had never seen
One whose pain did not last…What makes you different?
What makes you able to smile with those who you know have
Caused others to be victims?
Are you a victim or an angel?

I who have claimed to be so big, so bad and so bold, I could
Never do the things that you do, I could never say the words

That you say, if I had been treated anywhere close to the way
That you have been treated, I would still be seeking and searching
For that perfect revenge. But you, you embrace those who have
Hurt you, you smile at those who do not or cannot understand you,
And I bet that you even pray for those who hate you.
Are you a victim or an angel?

Although I hold that same cross so close to my chest, and it's meaning
I profess and confess, I cannot see or understand for the
Life of me, how you hold your heart so openly in your hand,
And allow it to love as if it had never been broken before.
Hate is just as strong of an emotion as love, what allows you to
Love so easily? What makes you so different?
I've seen and heard, heard and seen, so many of those self-pleasing
False messengers those who bring their imaginary messages from God
Oh yes, they say that God said love, love and give, give and love, or
Just give, give, give, just give. But you, you come into my
Existence without even knowing it, without the superficial tale of tales
The message that you brought was taught without the shifting
Of the spirits, or the wavering of a doubt.
Are you a victim or an angel?

I know that I could never be you, because you already have that
Job well fulfilled. So I'll do my part, before I got to sleep
Tonight, I'll pray to God in my own special way, I'll ask him to
Bless you, and to give you that extra strength that will be
Needed for you to smile one more day, as all his angels do.
And now I know for sure that you are not a victim,
Because you are definitely an Angel!

– Anonymous author, Wisconsin prison

There is no applause after this reading; an inmate says,

You are beautiful.

Would you put it in writing, Jackie teases.

What's the story behind the hat?

I wear a hat because I can wear a hat. The only time I won't, usually, is in the medium and maximum prisons. I wear a hat because I can and I dare you to try to take that hat.

There is laughter followed by a standing ovation for Jackie.

—————✕—————

There is a soothing sameness to these writing days on Isla Mujeres.
The peach sun rises early.
Green and red Navidad lights swing.
Groups of tourists sleep after their pulsing disco nights.
Roosters are stuck on *repeat*, always.
Dogs meander in packs.
Cats roam solo.
Golf carts, motorcycles and taxis scoot noisily.
I find coffee and email my sister.
People sweep.

—————✕—————

WILLOW RIVER BOOT CAMP, MINNESOTA · ANOTHER WINTER TALK

Jackie's second prison talk this day is at Willow River, a medium security facility – a *third generation* boot camp. There are learning opportunities in addition to the strict military regimen; in fact, educational programs are paramount. Physical training, military courtesy, and discipline are also basic. These men in the CIP (challenge incarceration program) can earn early release by successfully completing six months at Willow River followed by six months of intensive community supervision and then six months of monitored supervision. If they do not succeed, they return to prison to serve the full sentence without credit for their community time.

Many of these inmates have been involved in the manufacture, sale, or use of methamphetamines. Part of the intensive programming involves looking at the impact of their crimes on their victims and on the larger community. We are told that, as methamphetamine sales and use have increased in Minnesota, the age of people involved in first-degree drug crimes has also increased.

As we enter the gym, some men are gulping down their lunches while others quickly gather dishes and put away the tables and still others sweep. When lunch is finished, inmates march single file into the room. No one arrives late. Each of the ninety men carries a chair that is placed smartly in a circle while they stand at attention, hats folded over their arms, waiting for permission to sit. There is no talking. The only noise comes from the forced air heater. The director explained that, because of the success of this program, the facility is being doubled in size to house one hundred eighty men.

Nate, an instructor, asks the men, *What does restorative justice mean to you?*

Giving back, sir.

Going back into the community, sir.

To become a better and more positive person, sir.

How many think about what you have done every day?

All hands are abruptly raised.

The men wear military outfits. All their heads are shaved. They are 30, 40, 50, 60 years old.

Jackie is introduced and enters the circle of inmates. *On November 4, 1995…*

The mostly Caucasian men are watching Jackie walk. Acoustics are bad and a guard unplugs the soda machines and forced air heater. Jackie moves closer and closer to the men as she walks around inside the circle of chairs. I hear her right red shoe dragging on the cement floor. Sunlight from one high window lights some of the men's faces as if they are on stage.

Jackie's voice softens as she says, *I wake up to the world's toughest rehab schedule yet.* She has just spoken loudly about her sons' pain and anger.

The boys that did it to me and they were just boys…

The group is silent and attentive. All but two wear spit-shined black boots. The uniforms are tan. All wear white undershirts. All wear name badges to the left of their collars.

I watch a man about 30 as he listens to Jackie. She asks the question, *When can I receive parole? When can I see?* He shakes his head in mute response to her question. He continues to watch Jackie when she is on the other side of the group, but lowers his eyes, almost guiltily, as she passes close.

Jackie asks the men what they think she wanted from Craig after their first talk in prison.

An explanation, ma'am!

An apology, ma'am!

Why, ma'am!

Jackie listens to their responses and then says, *I asked him for a hug.*

Oh, my God! An older man blurts out involuntarily.

Like what a mother and a son do…

I thought about what Josh could do; he can't be here because he is in prison. He could write a letter…it is 2 pages. Who would want…

A man stands at attention. He reads to the letter, swiveling slowly as he reads. He appears professorial. He reads easily, well. He is comfortable in front of the group. He wears black plastic framed glasses that I later realize are prison issue. There are pauses in the reading, left for effect. He looks up at the dramatic points. He reads with expression. He is close to the ages of Jackie's sons.

Questions? Comments?

How long have you been in recovery, ma'am?

I have been in recovery every single day since. I walk. I do exercises for my hand and for my leg. I do them about five times a week. I don't want to go backwards. Jackie shrugs.

Ma'am, I try to put myself in the boys' position after trying to kill you. What do you talk about with them?

I wanted to meet them. I tried to guess why but they were just guesses. They are truly sorry. Jackie stands squarely in front of this young man, facing him. Both hands hang limply at her sides. She is fully vulnerable.

Ma'am, I would like to say that I am getting out of this that if you can forgive someone for trying to take your life, I should be able to forgive someone when I go out into the world after this. I thank you.

Ma'am, Did they get the maximum amount of sentence?

Craig got five years less than the maximum. The maximum was 70 for Josh, he got 65.

Ma'am, has Josh and Craig ever said "I love you" back?

Craig has told me he loves me. The first thing he does when he sees me is he hugs me like there is no tomorrow. Oh boy, oh boy.

Ma'am, You went through all the tribulations and beat a lot of the odds, what is some of the best advice you would give us. All of us are leaving within six months and we have a lot of odds stacked up against us.

You have a long row to hoe. You should be careful. You should think; think about each and every choice you have got and if that choice is good. The choice for Craig and Josh, it wasn't good. They could have walked away from it. I know that about 99.9% of you will never, never attempt murder. You will never do it. But decisions you have got; you should think, think about every single one of them and then you will make the right choice.

Ma'am, if they get paroled, will you let them in your house?

Yes.

Around your kids?

No. But I 100% know they won't hurt me again. I may live in a fairy tale world. But I know they won't hurt me ever again. You can disagree.

I'm not disagreeing, it is just unbelievable. It is unbelievable that you can just give.

I have a tape that is pretty good…

The men listen. I look above the VCR. There are banners on the concrete block walls, hung high. Names of the previous boot camp groups are listed: Delta, Alpha, Bravo, Foxtrot, Charlie, and Echo. The flags are decorated and names of inmates listed.

Applause.

Ma'am, I just don't know how you get all that heart in that little body.

I want you to write down the part about me having a little body. I like that. But I have a big heart.

Oh, there you go! The inmate smiles widely, fully.

Ma'am, sometimes you can hear a person speak and sometimes you can feel a person speak. What you have done today, I hear and feel what you are seeing. Here is something stuck. You make a person want to live and do right. I can sense that you were that kind of person even before. You have made my day.

Jackie walks toward the speaker, stops in front of him and, meaning every word, replies, *I am glad I have made your day.*

Ma'am, I will definitely reflect on this more. When little things are thrown at you – you have been through so much. I won't get so upset all the time. You have given me inspiration to turn some of the negatives into positives. I appreciate you coming.

Ma'am, you have been through a lot with this ordeal. You said you lost, and yes you have, but I have seen that you have gained more than you have lost. We are learning about empathy and compassion. Just seeing you today has gotten me thinking about what real compassion and real love are about. If you can go through what you have gone through and still have real love, even the little things that happen around here and in life, if you have love, you can move forward. Hatred hinders us. If we can just have a fraction of what you have.

Ma'am, I also want to say thank you. I am inspired by your courage and your wonderful heart. If you can be reborn again and have another chance at life, then

I know I can make it if I pay attention to you. What is it that you think about after each message?

With a nod, Jackie states, *I will continue to speak as long as I am on earth. You don't know, I will tell you, the bullet fragments are still in my head and they could kill me. Every day. Every day I am thankful, you know, that I haven't died yet! And I think they won't move. They won't move. And I will be able to speak.*

Ma'am, I just like to say we learned to be different people from this program. We write victim impact letters and things like that. You standing here in front of me today helps me see how my crime actually affected people in my life.

Prolonged clapping.

You get to go. I give you peace. Peace.

Thank you. Love you ma'am.

Standing ovation.

Nate stands again and speaks. *If you want to have any correspondence to Jackie you may do so through your caseworker.*

Yes sir, the men reply in unison.

Nate continues, *We have a lot of work to do for forgiving. You need to look at more than yourself; look at your victims. What have you learned?*

You need to be a productive member of society, sir.

Think about the victims, sir.

To help others you have to help yourself first, sir.

My choices, the choices I make are critical, sir.

Sir, even though we might go out there and do something wrong or real bad there is another person inside you that you can pull up from inside. When I leave these doors I will be a much better person.

I learned about spiritual being; if I let my spiritual being be in control I can be more than I am, Sir.

Application comes when you get into reentry, Sir.

Restorative justice is about love for community, family, self. If you don't know how to love you don't have anything, Sir.

AN INMATE'S LETTER

Dear Jackie:

Where to begin I am unaware. Words escape me on how much Jackie has influenced my life. Apart from God and my mother no one person has effected my life as Jackie has. I met Jackie a couple of years ago as I participated in the Reaching-Out group. The group was very helpful and important to the inmates and kids who were in it prior to her arrival, but after her arrival a spark was ignited. We never knew the victims point of view until Jackie came. The first meeting with Jackie was one of the hardest days in my life. Jackie stood up in front of 10 convicts and told her story to just us. No kids were around. When she was done I looked around and there wasn't a dry eye in the room. For 10 convicts to cry in a super max prison over a crime victim says a lot about Jackie. Jackie is honest and hopeful and above all the most forgiving lady I have ever met. As Jackie started attending our group every 2 weeks my bond with her grew stronger. At first all the other guys would hug her at the end when we were done. I never did until about a month after meeting her. I was raised in a house without a lot of affection so I felt uncomfortable. Jackie has a way of bringing out the good in all people. Jackie stood up with care and love and concern every two weeks and shared her pain with teens, just like the two that almost ended her life. God spared Jackies life as he did mine and I know God has a will for Jackie. Jackie stands up, half blind, half paralyzed and can make a grown man cry and really make them think, why? Why do we hurt others for no reason? Jackie has helped me overcome a lot of fears. She has brought me out of my shyness and taught me it is OK to cry. It's OK not to be strong all the time. Most people in society have an attitude of lock up criminals and throw away the key. If anyone should have this attitude it should be her but she is just the opposite. Jackie displays love and concern for all people. If there is any hope for the future, we have to look to people like her. I have been incarcerated for eight years and have had very few visits. After a while your family and friend desert you but I could always count on Jackie to be there to talk to and if I needed a hug she would give me one. One of the biggest ways Jackie affected my life was that she gave me the courage to meet face to face with my crime victims. I am a murderer and serving a life sentence. I did not have to meet my victims. I chose to because Jackie taught me love and forgiveness and that most crime victims want to know one question and that is *Why? Why did you commit this crime.* Wisconsin is a state that is now sending prisoners out of state and tearing apart families. If this madness is ever going to stop, Wisconsin or whomever needs to use people like Jackie. The best rehabilitation in the world I have found is to talk to your victims and people like Jackie. If the average convict doesn't understand the destruction he has done in someone's life, he will do it again. If we could follow Jackie's example of how to love each other and forgive people this world would be a much better place. I could write a hundred pages of stories I could share about Jackie on how she has made me cry and made me laugh. I am out of state in Tennessee right now and to not feel Jackie's hugs or see her smile is difficult. My advice to the State of Wisconsin and to whoever reads the book is to use people like Jackie to change men's lives and to stop the insanity of crime and its victims. To say Jackie is one of a kind is an understatement. Jackie's kids are blessed to have her for a mother and anyone who meets her will be changed for the better.

T, Wisconsin

AN EX-INMATE · THAD

Jackie and I have an appointment with Thad. During the years Thad was in prison, he and I were correspondents, writing each other about books, life, ideas and, as Mary Oliver says, *circling philosophies.*[13]

I forget my calendar and drive us to the wrong place. Jackie reminds me that we are to meet at the Einstein's bagel shop on the west end of Mineral Point Road. She is right and I tease her (and me) asking who it is who is supposed to have the memory loss around here.

While Jackie sips her Diet Coke, she explains briefly what happened to her. Thad listens politely, caringly.

---

[13] Oliver, Mary (1992). "Answers." *New and Selected Poems.* Boston: Beacon Press. P. 235.

Jackie turns her focus to Thad. *What prisons were you in?* She knows to use the plural in her question even though she and Thad have known each other for six minutes. The question isn't an affront. He understands it comes from her knowledge of a prison system that regularly moves inmates.

Dodge. Waupun; I was there for three years. Kettle Moraine and then to Jackson which is in Black River Falls.

Jackie asks, *How old are you?*

I'm 42 years old.

How many years did you have in prison?

I had a ten-year sentence. I did about 6 years and 6 months in prison and I was in the county jail about 9 months before.

If I may ask, what for? I am struck by the directness of both the questions and answers. No room for small talk.

Forgery, theft, bail-jumping, and two burglaries that I got put on probation for.

You have been out for about six months? You have turned your life around? I don't know the words to use. You are…are…out and you want to stay out.

Right. Thad nods. *The way I look at it is, during the time I was in prison I did a lot of work and thinking about myself. Now I live life as responsibly as I can. I take responsibility for everything I can. I engage in recovery-type programs. Voices Beyond Bars.[14] NA [Narcotics Anonymous] meetings. I have friends I talk to about things. I don't expose myself to anything that would lead to any irresponsible activity. It has not been difficult in that area. I have a lot of support. I did not*

---

[14] Voices Beyond Bars is a program of Madison Urban Ministry. From their website, the program is explained: *The number of former prisoners being released into our communities every year is growing. In the United States, there are about 170,000 newly released men and women in 1980. In 2005, that number will be over 650,000. Society is not prepared to receive these growing numbers of prisoners. In Wisconsin there are about 10,000 parolees and 22,000 prisoners. Two-thirds of those being admitted into Wisconsin prisons are going into prison because they were unsuc-*

spend my time in prison living in prison. I spent my time preparing to live outside prison. I actually live with two of my victims — my daughter and her mother. I victimized everyone who was connected to me. It is a thing I have to work on every day.

Do you find it is easy or hard?, Jackie poses.

Because I did the work for so long — training myself to engage in responsible behaviors — it isn't as hard as it would have been. I have struggles. I sometimes forget I am here to serve others, but I have to bring myself back and remember.

Jackie extends her hand toward where Thad's arms are resting on the table. *Don't lose sight of yourself. I have talked to hundreds and thousands of inmates. They — you know — sometimes they are thinking too much about themselves. They have to think about other people. But I would tell **you**, think about yourself. You have done things that are bad; you've done them. Now you have got to do the things that are good. I look at life differently than I did before. You talked about Voices Beyond Bars. That is stupendous. It is giving back to the community. I think that it is so good when I hear that an ex-inmate is giving back to the community. It is so good to do that. It is so important that you are giving back to your daughter and her mom.*

My daughter is 11.

Jackie turns to face Thad and smiles. *She is the apple of your eye?*

Thad's eyes crinkle with his big smile.

You realize that they were hurt? Thad nods again. *By it all?*

As a family we are still working on issues. My daughter forgives me. But she does not know if she can trust my presence in her life. She has difficulty even asking me certain things; little things like permission to get up to leave the table. She has grown to rely on her Mom.

---

cessful on probation or parole, not because of a new conviction. And Wisconsin is the number one state in the country for minority and teen-age incarceration per capita. Rebuilding a life after imprisonment is inherently challenging and everyone who succeeds benefits personally while adding to our community's well being. These programs have proven to reduce discrimination and increase former prisoner's civic participation.
http://www.emum.org/WhatWeDo/PrisonerReEntry.cfm

And Thad talks about the striving he is doing to make connections with the wider family.

You crossed a boundary, Jackie reflects.

Thad rests his arms on table, leaning toward Jackie as the restaurant begins to fill with chatting Saturday lunch goers. She is reaching toward his arms repeatedly. Their heads come closer together; their speech softens.

When I was in prison the biggest thing I learned was that I have to love myself.

And you did, didn't you?

I had to struggle with a lot around that area. I couldn't really love other people if I didn't love myself. But my actions didn't prove that to me So if I think that I am worthy of life and sharing life then I have to live a life that is respectful of myself and others.

The conversation moves to connections between the concepts of love and respect. Jackie reflects, *Inmates can say,* I love myself, *but I wonder if they really do love themselves. I have been in prisons; I have been in some of the worst prisons we have got. And the men there, their eyes looked straight down. I think because I respect them and they respect me.*

I think you are correct. Only, some people in prison don't know how to respect. Those people – I got to deal with a lot of people in prison because I taught basic skills – there were guys that really didn't have any care for themselves at all so they couldn't care for others. The word respect in prison means, I won't mess with you. *Respect is a huge issue in prison. But I do believe guys come to see you because you have a very powerful aura.*

Her head tilted, Jackie says, *I have heard that before. I don't understand.*

It is a clean feeling that you get off of a person. That is the way I get it. A person…a lot of stuff happens to people in life and they become blemished. If you can forgive, your light is cleaned. It shines. You have a bright light.

Wow. I am very proud of you for coming out of prison and stepping up to the plate and being a father and being there for your fiancée and working the job and driving the car. It is good.

Do you know how powerful that is that you talk with the inmates?, Thad asks. *What you are doing? Seeing those guys – just the energy that comes to them. Do you get that from them, how powerful that is?*

I do. I talk and about 95% of them will listen to me and I hope they will take it back and think about it. I don't yell. I don't scream. I talk to them.

A pause and then Thad adds, *This has been one powerful week for me; I am working to allow myself to be open to life.*

You have got to take off your blinders. In prison you got blinders. You have got to take them off and see life as it is. I am an eternal optimist and I am trying to get everybody to learn. I believe in you. I believe that you can do whatever you want. It has been very nice to meet you. I wish you peace, Jackie concludes.

As they say in Ghost, *Ditto,* Thad replies with a smile.

MUSINGS
PRIOR TO A TALK WITH MARQUETTE UNIVERSITY LAW STUDENTS

Jackie is standing at the podium as she speaks to the empty lecture classroom in the Marquette University Sensenbrenner Law School and Library.

We are waiting together for her presentation in the room next door; waiting for the law students to return from a break in their day-long class. Mostly, Jackie doesn't directly address me though I am the only other person in the room. Her candid reflections tell me we have moved beyond our inauspicious beginning to this writing project when she told me she would not allow me "into her mind."

Just for a few minutes, her optimistic shield is down. As I listen, she talks herself through the momentary sadness, aloud – a micro pity-party perhaps. It feels as if I am seeing directly into her mind. And I also see the gift her audiences bring; the healing they give her.

*I will tell you that I don't remember my **sons' graduations** – graduations from middle school, from high school, from college. That is **hard**. I can't remember **holding** my sons when they were babies. I can't remember holding **my sons**. I **must** have held my sons. Is it because I don't want to* *remember what **I don't have** or is it because I just **don't** remember? I don't know.*

*My legs feel like they are **heavy** today; they are **painful** to the 10th degree – 100 pins. I am a little dizzy. I get to feeling sorry for myself and I don't like it but sometimes I do feel sorry for myself.*

*But I can **walk**! I am **out** of a wheelchair. A five-legged cane? I had that for a time. I graduated to a seeing-eye cane. But around the house I don't have a cane. I can walk **straight lines**. I can walk to the **left**. I can walk **straight** ahead. I can walk to my **right**. These are all things I have worked up to. You don't even have one **fathom** of understanding.*

Turning to face me directly, Jackie continues, *Your **sister** does. I say your sister because I think she will know what I am talking about.* My mind pauses and visualizes the muscle degenerative disease that continues to clip my sister's wings, as she would say.

Turning back to the empty room, Jackie continues her soliloquy. *You are a **gift-ed** person. You can walk. My sister, my kids are **gifted** people. They can walk. If I could walk how I used to, how **proud** I would be. To walk the way most people do; I **marvel** at that. The times I stop. I rest my legs. I rest my arm. I rest my eyes. I say I **rest** and most people say,* Oh, you rest. *No, **I REST**!*

*I am not **jealous** that they can walk and I have trouble. But what I know is I will **never walk normally**. I will **never see normally**. I will **never talk normally**. I will do everything as normally as I can. I am **not** saying it for **pity**. I am telling them the **truth**. I don't want their arm to help me walk. That **burns** me; it **invades** my space – because I **can** do it – a bit slower, a bit haltingly, but I **do** it.*

*I can understand. Before I was hurt, I must have been in a **hurry**. I would like them to **stop** and smell the flowers. There are too many people rushing. You know, driving a car – someone will **beep** at me or they will say something towards me. They have **got** to stop it. I just about got **hit** crossing Segoe Road. It was my turn to walk and I started walking and a car went through a red light, went speeding past me and **scared** me. That scared me so much I **cried**. I went back. I **stayed** back. And all of the rest of the cars stopped for me. The light was green for them to go, but **they stayed stopped for me**.*

*I am tired of hearing people say **they know**. They **don't** unless you have it going on in **your** life.*

She pauses and I tell her a short story about my sister. *When I was visiting one time, my sister and I were doing some cleaning in her kitchen. She wanted the high cupboards cleaned and couldn't reach them. I simply pulled a chair over and climbed up on it; an act that was easy and not physically challenging in any way. She watched me and I saw her watching me, remembering that she couldn't do what I had just, unthinkingly done. She smiled at me as we both understood. She said,* Show off!

Jackie smiles and gestures to her feet. Earlier I commented on the bright red shoes she is wearing. *I purchased the shoes 18 months ago,* she explains, softening.

***These** are the first flat shoes I've owned since the accident. They are fashionable but don't provide the same support the high shoes do. I shouldn't have worn these shoes today; should have worn my high top shoes. I wore these because I'm speaking to a group of adults. I wanted to be as much **like** them as humanly possible. These are **spiffy**. They **hurt** my feet; my foot. I know that I am going to hurt when I wear them and hurt I will be. It's about mind over matter. I will be **normal** for the hours that I wear them. I used to go barefoot all the time before the accident. I would go barefoot in the winter at home. But not now. I wear my high tops and that is normal to me.*

*I would like to **click** my **heels** together and **wish** that my **foot** would be **normal**. I would like Craig and Josh to have to **wear my red shoes**. They would **laugh** at it. I know with my **head** that I can't wear low tops, but my **heart** is the problem.*

*I watch people run and jump. I want to do that but if I did I'd be **flat** on my face. I would look **insanely stupid**.*

*To sit down, I have to have a chair that is pulled out. I **sit** on the **side** of the chair arm and then turn myself to **slide** in. Others can sit on a chair normally. I would give you a **million dollars** if I could sit in a chair normally.*

*I have watched how people get into a car. I have noticed their right leg is the first to go in. It amazes me **how the leg** goes in the **car**. Whereas, when I do it, it is sitting down with **both** feet on the ground, on the outside, and then **swinging** my legs around. It **amazes** me that people can **do** it the other way. You know, when I get* *out of the chair I have to put the weight on my left side and I do it that way. That is a way for me.*

I look normal standing here but I take my **first** *step and I'm* **not** *normal.*

How do you **drive** *a car?* The question is rhetorical; Jackie continues.

I know **one** *pedal is for* **gas** *and* **one** *for the* **brake.** *I* **don't** *know how to use them. I know you have turn signals. I ask which side the signals are on and am told. Someone might tell me and* **tomorrow** *I won't know. I know you can* **turn** *the wheel. But I don't know* **how** *you turn the wheel to go right or to go left. I have* **forgotten,** *I* **think** *I have forgotten how to do it. I think that I am in* **awe** *of someone driving because I used to drive; I used to drive very well. I don't feel badly; I feel in* **awe.**

Putting on **lipstick?** *It intrigues me. I put on lipstick but I don't* **see** *because* **my face is blank** *in the mirror, except for hair. I know how to put powder on my face. I know how to put cream on my face. I know how to do it,* Jackie laughs, *but it is a joke because I don't see. I say,* I can **see** – **except for my blind spots.** *I use my left hand and I put on the lotion on my face and hands and on my feet. I put my face three inches from the mirror and I do put on lipstick.*

But I won't color my hair. *That would be* **asking** *for it.*

I am **thankful** *for so many things – that my sweater was put on the right way. I feel for the tag. I know that the tag should be in the back. My jeans. I know that the front opens.* **If you only knew,** *if you only knew the* **talks** *I have with* **myself.** *I hope that I'm wearing everything the right way; if I'm not, I am an* **imbecile.** *Then I take it off and* **start** *over again.*

My **dentist** *is proud of me. I don't have* **any** *cavities. I don't have anything wrong. But he doesn't know that I take the time; I* **brush** *my teeth, I* **floss** *my teeth. I take* **mouthwash.** *I do* **everything** *he asks so I won't have a filling. A filling is bad news for me. After the accident I became* **kind of afraid of needles.** *Before then it was a snap but after, I've had so many needles – so many needles. I wouldn't even count them.*

It is the **little things** *that I wish I could do. You take* **eating** *for granted. I* **cannot** *take it for granted. I hope the food* **gets** *to my mouth so I can take a bite. I have* **everything** *set up. My glass sits in the 10 or 11 o'clock position. My napkin is on* *the left of the plate. I know that I have a sandwich; it is on the left. Whatever else I have to eat is on the right. I **can't** have them mixed up. Somebody would say, You are repetitive. **I have to be repetitive.***

*I have to go in the bathroom and take my toothbrush out. The toothbrush is facing the sink. The floss is to the right of the toothbrush. It **has** to be. I know there is the towel when you wash your hands. Then there is the towel when you wash your hair. There is a towel to wash off my glasses and another towel for my body. If a person went in and put the towels willy nilly, I would be **lost.***

*When I make my bed I make it **the same every time**. I hang the sheet just below the mattress. I do the sheet. I walk around. I do the sheet on the other side. I do the quilt on that side. I put the pillow on the right side. I go around and do the same thing on the left.*

*It is always the **same** so I will know what I've done. It might be **funny** to others but **not** to me.*

*I was on vacation in Florida by myself. I thought I would walk by myself. I thought the walk was all one level. I was wrong. I found out when I fell down four or five stairs. I said to myself, **never again**, never again am I going on vacation. But I got over it. You should see I had bloody fingers, knee, foot; I was a mess. But it was my **ego** that was **hurt** the most. Now I know I will take my cane and feel out where I am. I will take **two** canes.*

*I have **trouble** talking when I get **excited**. My brain makes me **lethargic** and I have **no control** over my speech or my walking. When I get excited, say I was going on vacation, I would become like a **blubbering idiot**. I would try to talk; I **could not**. I would try to walk; I **couldn't**. I could walk, but on my **ankle**. Everything, my walking, my talking, it becomes very **garbled** so that **a normal person could not understand me**.*

*I don't eat at home mainly because **I don't want to** eat at home. It is a time to **meet** people. Eating out is something I can do. It is **good** for me. It is good to be in the mainstream of people. If left alone, I would be a **recluse**.*

***I constantly talk because I have to talk.** I think that I would become a non-talking individual if I didn't talk. So many people will say, they know what I mean but I want to say it myself.*

*I really can't cook because the **oven would do me in**; I would forget I have it on. But I **can** do the dishwasher. There were times that I didn't do a thing. That was lazy of me. Someone would say, You deserve to be lazy. That is **hogwash**. It is hard work to do the things I need to do. I think I am **not** lazy. I've got to get in to do more things. I think I am **a very smart individual** and I can figure out how to do certain things.*

It is nearly time for Jackie to begin speaking to the group. I feel the intensity of her emotion and her irritation softening as she has talked herself through it, aloud.

*I would like to have Craig and Josh **be** with me for one week and they would have to **see** everything I do. It isn't that I would like them to walk in my shoes – well, **maybe my RED shoes** – it is seeing what I **have** to do day in and day out.*

*Craig, bless his heart, wrote me a letter yesterday and he told me of all of the **injustices** he's had – on four pieces of paper.*

There is a long pause; I remain quiet. Jackie continues. *I've had **injustices**. Granted, you have injustice in prison. I will not tell you they don't. But I have injustice from the time I wake up until the time I go to bed. I look out and... for instance, I went to my favorite place to eat – Hong Kong Café. I took out my money and gave it to the cashier. I thought I gave her a $20. It was a $10. And I asked her if I hadn't given her a $20 and she said no. I went back to her later and I said, I am so sorry, I am legally blind. I thought I gave you a $20. In this world of hurry up, hurry up, hurry up, when you buy something and when you have given them your money and get back your change, it is hurry up. I **can't** hurry up. And so I jam the change in my purse. I don't put it in the wallet like I should.*

*That is a small tale of the injustices. I would like Craig and Josh to go with me for a week, not to **say** anything – not to say **anything** – but to watch me when I give the woman what I thought was a $20 and it is $10. That **mortifies** me. It is like someone standing and **beating** me –* Jackie gestures a flogging with her hand – *making me understand that I'm disabled.*

*I don't **think** that I am disabled. **That** is the problem. That is **my** problem. I am disabled until I die.*

*I used to say give me 24 hours of me being normal but 24 would become 48, would become 72 and so on and so on. I know. So I don't ask for the time of being normal. **I am disabled.** I was hurt by Craig and Josh. But I **am making my way** in a sight-filled society.*

The instructor for the Marquette University class appears in the doorway and motions to Jackie. It is time to speak to his students.

Jackie finishes: *I am making my way. It is my **little life** in the moment – **I have a life of moments.** I celebrate them. I say I am **stubborn.** I mean **I AM STUB-BORN.** Oh, boy, am I stubborn. The stubbornness has got me here. **Yes it has. Yes it has. Yes it has.** Because I am Jackie Millar!*

She walks into the classroom. Thirty future attorneys sit with their chairs in a circle. *I am Jackie Millar and I am alive. I am healed from within. I am at peace.*

━━◦✕◦━━

Jackie: My name is Monique and I am 17 years old.
I am currently a senior in high school. I admire you so much;
your story touched more than my heart it touched my soul.
It is so strange how one stupid mistake can change your whole life.
I am happy that you forgave Craig and Josh but I am not happy
about all the pain and suffering you had to go through.
For your children, my heart goes out to them.
You are more than my inspiration you are my guardian angel.

Love always, M

━━◦✕◦━━

WRITING JOURNAL

Jackie's emotional memory of the shooting is inexorably connected with John's house. In a similar way for me, the final editing of this story will forever be connected with Isla Mujeres.

On the island, the days are twelve hours long. The nights are twelve hours long. It is literally a world of light and dark.

We dichotomize many things. Yin and yang. The world as it is vs. the world as it should be. The local and the global. Jackie's story reminds me that life is more complex than that. It is a paradoxical, contradictory, mind-bending, shimmering mix.

I think of Craig's painful, stressed description of the interior of the candy apple red Honda as a metaphor for the complexity of life.

It's got like gray interior and it's like the seats are kind of darkish-lightish gray, not that dark and not like the steering wheel and all the like rubber and plastic and stuff so they're really dark gray, almost like a black. He continued, That's about it unless you want, if you really want me to get into detail on it, I can.

Jackie sees red…and bright yellow and green and gray. She is vulnerable and independent. She mourns her losses and celebrates her life. She hates the cruel acts of two boys that have changed her life, their lives and the lives of so many others forever. And she forgives the boys.

She loves the boys. Jackie has taught me that the world is a rainbow that we must seize each day. She invites us all to seize the day and do as she does, *to know that we are alive.*

On my final day on the island, I take a holiday. I rent a wobbly golf cart and drive to the south point of Isla Mujeres. There stands a tiny Mayan Temple ruin – a woman's temple. The site is a wonderful windy point where waves smash noisily into high cliffs, frigate birds are suspended and the aquamarine Caribbean Sea shimmers. There is a plaque near the ruins succinctly explaining the site.

The words read: Mayan Temple to Goddess Ixchel…Lady Rainbow…

Perhaps Jackie is Lady Rainbow.

TO MY MOM:
BY DEREK MILLAR

Ten years… How long ago, but yet so painfully fresh in memory. This was the day everything changed for all who know and love you. But most importantly this was the last day of your old life and, at the same time, a new beginning. I couldn't begin to understand the depth of feelings you'll experience on November 4, 2005; but I'm certain it will be an intense and emotional day.

I love you Mom. I have so much to thank you for and be proud of. You experienced something most people never will. You overcame the deepest physical and emotional wounds and responded with a new life of genuine love and passionate service. The events of the last decade have taught me about the awesome might of God as well as your character. The following is a tribute to you:

November Fourth of '95
The day that time stood still.
When evil forced its senseless hand
Upon a mother's will.
But let me tell you of the tale
And of this woman strong;
And you will be astonished
By the right that came from wrong.

It all began on rural land
Amidst the evergreens.
A harmless spot, a tree-filled lot,
Involving troubled teens.
The kids arrived, hell-bent for fun
Perhaps a car and cash?
But did they know about the life

They were about to dash?
The shot rang out, a vicious act.
The kind you won't forgive.
But this story ends differently.
Her only way to live.

The wounds were deep, a fragile life.

She barely made it through.
Her loving family and her friends
Unsure of what to do.

But did she ever beat the odds.
In fact she proved them wrong.
Returned from death and sharing life
Became her mission song.
A newfound second chance to live.
Albeit not the same.
She visits prisons, talks to kids
Despite her damaged frame.

There is a message here for us
Beyond this frightening day.
A woman had her life torn down
So she could claim to say,
"Your life can be an awesome one
If you should choose to live
With the heart of God within your soul
And the power to forgive."

So Mom, I offer this to you.
I'm proud of who you are.
The path was steep, your pain so deep,
The road you traveled far.

Instead I see that smile of yours,
Excitement in your voice.
To stand up strong or hide in fear?
You've shown us all your choice.

God bless this special day, Mom. I truly love you now more than ever.
Your Proud Son, Derek

WHAT I SEE

BY JACKIE MILLAR

The dew gets settled in the grass all around,
The sun makes its presence known,
The animals are in the trees, in the water, and in the grass, all around,
The trees with their branches out-stretched as if they touch the moon,
The flowers are so beautiful and fragrant as they dance all 'round.
The lakes are doing their thing as they only know how to do it.

That scene plays for me every day!
You ask me why that scene plays every day for me?
I answer it plays the same scene for me, because I am legally blind!
There is silence from you,

I ask you, Why are you silent,
You answer, It is because you are blind.
You say it with such sadness.
Maybe I should look at my blindness differently,
But I don't. I look at it as God's way of looking at things differently.

To me, the scene plays the same way, time after time,
Beautiful, serene, uncomplicated, all perfectly in tune,
I may be legally blind, but I see with my heart!

BONUS TRACK AUDIO CD

JACKIE'S SONG

(LeMaire, Cryner, Blazy, Stults)

A Hard Day S Write Music, Careers BMG Music, EMI Blackwood Music
Ensign Music, Lonesome Dove Music, Ticket To Ride Music

Sung by **Teresa James**
Produced by **Mike Stults**

G●LDEN™

Copyright © ℗ 2007 Golden, The Record Label
PO Box 17103 • Encino, CA 91416 • 818-708-9488